Economic Competition in the 21st Century

HOWARD J. SHATZ

Prepared for the United States Air Force
Approved for public release; distribution unlimited

RAND | PROJECT AIR FORCE

For more information on this publication, visit www.rand.org/t/RR4188

Library of Congress Cataloging-in-Publication Data is available for this publication.
ISBN: 978-1-97740-0547-0

Published by the RAND Corporation, Santa Monica, Calif.
© Copyright 2020 RAND Corporation
RAND® is a registered trademark.

Support RAND
Make a tax-deductible charitable contribution at
www.rand.org/giving/contribute

www.rand.org

Preface

The U.S. government is devising international policies under the principle that the United States faces growing political, economic, and military competition. This report discusses different forms of economic competition, including the concept of national competitiveness, competition for markets and investment, the use of economic tools in other realms of international competition, and competition over the nature of the global economic system. The results of this competition have direct and indirect relevance to the U.S. armed forces, most important by enabling the funding of the personnel, equipment, and technology the armed forces use, but also by influencing the global security environment.

Research conducted for this report is part of a broader Project AIR FORCE project that examines the nature of international competition; evaluates its military, economic, geopolitical, and informational components; and assesses the perspectives of the major powers. The research reported here was commissioned and sponsored by the Director of Strategy, Concepts, and Assessments, Deputy Chief of Staff for Strategic Plans and Requirements, and conducted within the Strategy and Doctrine Program of RAND Project AIR FORCE as part of a fiscal year 2018 project, *America and Strategic Competition in the 21st Century*, that assists the Air Force with executing its Strategic Master Plan.

This report should be of value to the national security community and interested members of the general public, especially those with an interest in competition in the international economy, the future of the international system, and the U.S. role in dealing with rising competition.

RAND Project AIR FORCE

RAND Project AIR FORCE (PAF), a division of the RAND Corporation, is the U.S. Air Force's federally funded research and development center for studies and analyses. PAF provides the Air Force with independent analyses of policy alternatives affecting the development, employment, combat readiness, and support of current and future air, space, and cyber forces. Research is conducted in four programs: Strategy and Doctrine; Force Modernization and Employment; Manpower, Personnel, and Training; and Resource Management. The research reported here was prepared under contract FA7014-16-D-1000.

Additional information about PAF is available on our website:
www.rand.org/paf

The draft report, issued in April 2019, was reviewed by formal peer reviewers and U.S. Air Force subject-matter experts.

Contents

Figures and Tables

Figures

Tables

Summary

U.S. foreign policy is being built around a fundamental assumption that the United States faces growing competition around the world. This competition is occurring in the political and military realms, but also in the economic realm—a realm of direct and indirect relevance to the strength of the U.S. armed forces and the global security environment. This report discusses economic competition from a number of different perspectives. These include ideas about national competitiveness, competition for markets and investment, the use of economic tools in other realms of competition, economic warfare, and competition over the nature of the global economic system. These different perspectives may be placed in two broad groups: competition as outcome and competition as action.

Competition involves two or more parties contending for some scarce goal with the outcome being that one of the parties will enhance its power or influence relative to another. This report, and the RAND Corporation project on Strategic Competition of which it is a part, have adopted the following broad definition of competition: *Competition in the international realm involves the attempt to gain advantage, often relative to others believed to pose a challenge or threat, through the self-interested pursuit of contested goods such as power, security, wealth, influence, and status.* Research for this report was concluded in October 2019.

Strategic Competition in Economics

The idea of strategic competition among nations is embedded in a long-running debate among economists about competitiveness. The issue enters into the realm of strategic competition among nations because one view holds that competitiveness relates to the global market position of a national industry. In the United States in the late 1980s and early 1990s, this pertained largely to the global position of high-technology industries.

For most economists, national economic competitiveness is now taken to mean the ability to spur increases in productivity and standards of living, with a focus on domestic economic policies, and can be considered competition as outcome; all nations can institute policies to increase productivity and standards of living, such as by improving educational systems, without directly affecting each other. However, there is disagreement about the idea of global technology leadership and the proper role, if any, of government action to encourage that. Such disagreements focus on which institutions, policies, and factors governments should support, ranging from support for broadly beneficial institutions and policies to support for specific technologies or economic sectors.

Economic Competition Beyond Competitiveness

Countries conduct economic competition in a number of different ways, beyond ensuring their economies are "competitive." They compete for export markets and inward foreign direct investment (FDI), echoing eighteenth-century mercantilism in which trade surpluses were seen as a goal to foster economic growth and state power. Often, they do so through subsidized finance or through other forms of direct assistance. They also compete to develop leadership in technology-intensive industries. After the fact, it is possible to see which countries host the dominant firms in a technology area and where the most technologically advanced products come from. But even more than with exports or investment, tracing the pathway from government action to technological dominance is difficult, and policies to boost technology-intensive industries often fare poorly or do not improve the broader economy. Finally, countries compete to make sure standards that are favorable to their industries are adopted more widely. These may come in the form of regulatory requirements or technical standards.

The final arbiter of technology leadership or successful competition in the global economy remains the ability of a country to foster domestic economic growth with a level of inequality that is politically tolerable. Despite a great focus on international competition, domestic economic policies regarding such mundane matters as efficient government spending, effective training programs, and sensible regulatory regimes retain primacy in affecting economic power and success.

Geopolitical Competition with Economic Tools

Economics as a field of competition involves not only the search for growth and markets. It also includes using economic tools to further geopolitical goals—competition as action. These uses have been come to be known by some analysts and policymakers as *geoeconomics*. This is not the use of economic tools to improve a nation's economy. Rather, it is the use of economic instruments to support other goals, including defending national interests and producing more favorable political, diplomatic, or security outcomes.

In the area of punishment, these tools include the use of sanctions to cause policy change, destabilize a government, stop a country from acting, or send a message to other nations or the public. Such actions can include a broad variety of sanctions on trade, investment, finance, and people. At a more aggressive level, using economic actions to coerce can accumulate to become economic warfare. The line between the two is not distinct, but economic warfare would include economic actions to achieve not just economic but military and geopolitical goals. Although the goals of economic warfare are different from the goals of economic competition, many of the tools are the same. Economic warfare can include trade and investment limits, travel bans, and in the case of actions instituted by the United States, limits on the use of the U.S. financial system. But economic warfare can go well beyond these tools and include blockades of ports, bombing of factories, or cyberattacks on political or military targets, and it may include covert actions.

Economic tools can also be used to reward. Countries and institutions around the world provide more than $225 billion in official development assistance, including grants or loans on concessional financial terms offered by governments to promote economic development or welfare. Such aid can be helpful in achieving those goals. Although generally frowned on by aid advocates and development officials, aid has always had foreign policy goals that can be viewed through the lens of strategic competition. Goals have included winning allegiance to and obtaining favorable treatment for the donor country. In addition, despite the apparent generosity, aid can have negative consequences, both for development and in achieving political goals.

Competition over the System Itself

A final major area in which countries compete is in setting the rules under which they compete economically, specifically, the rules of the global trade, investment, and finance system. These rules can also have geopolitical effects in the way they create norms of behavior and how they influence political systems. The rules-based international economic system established following World War II has rested on three main pillars. The first is multilateral trade liberalization through what was originally the General Agreement on Tariffs and Trade and is now the World Trade Organization. The second is assistance originally for balance-of-payments adjustments and later for all manner of financial and budget crises under the International Monetary Fund. The third is economic development under the World Bank and regional development banks.

These pillars have supported two simple ideas that have been implemented slowly: International trade and investment should be free among nations, with benefits that are accorded to one partner accorded to all. Furthermore, businesses of one nation operating in another, either through trade or investment, should be afforded the same treatment as the local businesses in the nation in which they are operating.

As with many other aspects of global economics, the effect of China's growing role in the world economy has the potential to change the institutional foundations of international trade and investment. The most contentious area affecting the system is China's efforts to make international institutions accommodate its state-led economic system on an equal basis to market economies. Gaining greater acceptance for state-led economies within the international system could have strongly negative effects on that system.

Economic Competition and the Armed Forces

Beyond the well-being of a country's population and growth of a country's economy and production capacity, economic competition is relevant to the armed forces. The wealth and output generated by economic activity leads directly to the ability of a nation to fund the personnel, equipment, and operations of the armed forces and the technological development that can lead to more effective weapons and operations. To the extent that economic competition, however defined, leads to a larger economy, economic competition can enable larger, more powerful armed forces and underpin increased chances of victory in wartime.

The changing nature of defense procurement also demonstrates the links between economic competition and the armed forces. Reliance on commercial off-the-shelf technology has increased, not only because much of the innovation is taking place in commercial activities but also because buying from the commercial market (or modifying commercial products) can be cheaper than buying custom-made technology. A stronger economy can fund not only the research, development, and manufacturing activities that result in new technology, but the education and training that provide the workforce and knowledge for the development of that technology.

One other factor that makes economic competition highly relevant for the armed forces is that international security interests may follow international economic interests. This is particularly a concern with China's growth and internationalization. Already, China is the leading trade partner of many countries. As trade and financial orientation changes, political orientation could follow. Additionally, China may want to expand its military presence to protect its investments and Chinese nationals working throughout the world. Such activities are not yet a security challenge for the United States but may become so.

Policy Implications of Economic Competition

Countries are competing economically in a variety of ways and using economic tools to compete in security and geopolitical domains. Does this economic competition matter? One way to answer the question is to start with what countries are competing for, how they compete, and whether global competition allows them to meet their goals (Table S.1).

One view of economic competition is reflected in the 1990s debates about *competitiveness*, in which countries compete to offer their residents a decent standard of living and job opportunities. But another way to frame this idea is that countries are endeavoring to create a policy environment that offers residents the chance to have a decent standard of living and job opportunities, and so this is not really much of a competition because it can be positive-sum (both parties may gain from competition) rather than zero-sum (one party gains and the other party loses just as much) and all countries could achieve these goals. Achieving these goals is best served through smart domestic economic policy. Accordingly, the policy implication is that policymakers should focus on providing stable fiscal and monetary policies that emphasize long-run economic growth to undergird the overall economic and political strength of the nation.

Countries are competing to open markets for their companies and attract investment. In some cases, this competition is zero-sum. Investment and trade mean little on their own, but they can contribute to domestic prosperity and opportunity, so such competition matters. They are also working to ensure the standards that favor their companies are the internationally accepted standards; doing so will enhance the ability of their companies to operate internationally.

The higher-profile competition is for leadership in industries making and using new technologies. Certainly, government policy and support can create new, leading industries.

Table S.1. Domains of Economic Competition

Domain	Typical Tools	Economic Effect	Assessment
Economic warfare	Sanctions, blockades, and attributed or unattributed attacks on economic targets to achieve economic, military, and political goals	Degrading or destroying an adversary's economic capacity can reduce that adversary's freedom of action	Use of economic warfare is an adjunct to other types of warfare and by itself will rarely achieve military or political goals, at least over the short to medium term
International economic leverage	Foreign aid for the purpose of gaining allies or winning specific policy debates; economic sanctions to shape behavior; other tools for geopolitical purposes	Evidence that these tools can shape behavior, but economic consequences uncertain	Sanctions can be effective in specific cases but often fail to achieve goals; aid leverage mixed; other tools may have high costs
Leading and setting rules of the system	Helping to found and set rules of international economic institutions; issuing global reserve currency; dominating standards-setting organizations; predominant voting share in institutions; leading voice in informal forums	Limited evidence, but available cases suggest system structure can benefit leader and participants	Some systemic roles (reserve currency, leading institutions) provide major competitive advantages
Public-sector competitiveness policies	Public-sector funding of research and development; support for specific industries; national technology and industrial strategies; public-private partnerships	Evidence that broader policies, at least, can generate economic strength	Overall innovation-system investment can make a difference, but targeted, state-led policies can misidentify winners and losers
Domestic economic fundamentals	Fiscal responsibility and health; stable, effective monetary policy; regulatory and tax environment; rules and standards that affect innovation; socioeconomic opportunity; domestic institutions that support effective economic policy	Clear, consistent evidence that these policies are essential to economic strength	The foundation for all effective competition; other areas will not make up for failures in these areas

SOURCE: Author's assessment based on research for this report.
NOTE: The table presents the different categories of economic competition, whether the purpose is more to provide for domestic economic strength or to serve as tools of geopolitical competition, and a brief note on their effectiveness.

Evidence suggests that much more is needed to achieve broad prosperity, such as national innovation systems and the country's receptivity to absorb and use new technologies. Both of these are far harder to create, support, and sustain. This suggests that policymakers should institute general innovation-supporting policies, such as promoting infrastructure, basic research, patent protections, and technology development to support overall competitiveness, and should avoid attempting to pick specific winners and losers in sectors or companies.

Where competition is most likely to matter is in setting the rules by which countries trade, invest, and conduct financial transactions globally. As of 2019, that was largely a Western-derived system, featuring equal treatment of foreign companies, the application of tariffs and barriers on a nondiscriminatory basis, and accepted methods of dispute resolution. But with countries instituting trade barriers, the United States trying to renegotiate certain aspects of the global trading system, and China appearing to wait for a time to remake the global system when the current system no longer serves its interests, the overall system is under pressure (although still far freer than it was through most of history and even the post–World War II era). In some ways, Europe is caught in the middle—finding common commercial cause with the United States vis-à-vis China but finding common institutional cause with China vis-à-vis the United States in the desire to uphold global economic institutions, at least for now.

Knowledge of which countries have succeeded in competition for specific markets can be gained just by looking at which companies have the largest market share for an industry. Technological leadership is harder to gauge, but such measures as patents and, more important, sales by technology companies can shed light on that. Gauging the results of competition for the overall system is still more difficult, but possible. For that, the issue will be whether the basic principles of free exchange and fair treatment that have been promoted since just after the end of World War II will be maintained or whether systems favoring significant state intervention and selective barriers and treatment will emerge. From a policy perspective, U.S. policymakers should take advantage of the relative size of the U.S. economy to set rules for the international system that are conducive to the U.S. economy and attractive to other countries in the long run.

Geopolitical competition using economic tools can be effective, but the use of such tools can also be costly. Through restraints or new regulations on business, the use of these tools is trading off economic performance for geopolitical objectives. In addition, through overuse, economic tools could lead targeted countries to create alternative systems or workarounds, not only blunting their power but potentially diminishing the economic performance of the country using the tools in the first place. Accordingly, as with any other geopolitical tool, policymakers should weigh their costs against their benefits and use them judiciously. For the United States, at least for now and likely through the next decade, if not longer, economic tools are likely to remain effective.

Finally, tools of economic warfare can prove destructive to an adversary's economy, but there is little evidence that by themselves they achieve military or political goals when an adversary's core interests are at stake, at least in the short to medium term. They can also invite similar actions in retaliation, a particular concern when aimed at a large economy with which the United States might be interdependent. Furthermore, they can have consequences for noncombatants, including loss of life. Policymakers should treat the tools of economic warfare as they would any other instrument of war, assessing positive strategic effect and potential harm before deploying them.

In geopolitical competition and warfare, economic tools can serve as an adjunct to U.S. military power; the ability to use them provides one example of why economic competition is relevant to the armed forces. More broadly, economic competition and its goals of positive domestic economic performance have relevance to the armed forces as well. More direct effects include the ability of the United States to appropriately fund its defense and provide the armed forces with the personnel, equipment, and technology needed to protect the United States from present and future challenges. This places economic competition as an essential element in consideration of overall strategic competition, relevant to military and defense planners.

Acknowledgments

The author thanks Paula Thornhill, former director of the RAND Project AIR FORCE Strategy and Doctrine Program, and Michael J. Mazarr, project leader for *America and Strategic Competition in the 21st Century*, for their support and detailed comments throughout the research, and Raphael S. Cohen, associate director of the Strategy and Doctrine Program in Project AIR FORCE, for valuable comments on early drafts. Meetings with government officials and experts at research organizations in London, Brussels, Berlin, and Warsaw added context and a variety of useful perspectives. Formal reviews from Michael J. Meese and Steven W. Popper and additional comments from James Dobbins greatly strengthened the manuscript. Thanks go also to the project sponsor, U.S. Air Force A5/8, for support and overall guidance. Julienne Ackerman guided publication as the production editor, and external editorial partner Karen Brogno provided expert copyediting assistance. Together, they strengthened the manuscript. All errors of fact and interpretation are the responsibility of the author.

Abbreviations

AI	artificial intelligence
CPTPP	Comprehensive and Progressive Trans-Pacific Partnership
EPO	European Patent Office
EU	European Union
FDI	foreign direct investment
FRED	Federal Reserve Economic Data
GATT	General Agreement on Tariffs and Trade
GDP	gross domestic product
IMF	International Monetary Fund
IP	intellectual property
IPR	intellectual property rights
JPO	Japan Patent Office
MFN	most-favored nation
OECD	Organisation for Economic Co-operation and Development
PCAST	President's Council of Advisors on Science and Technology
PPP	purchasing-power parity
RCEP	Regional Comprehensive Economic Partnership
TPP	Trans-Pacific Partnership
TTIP	Transatlantic Trade and Investment Partnership
USAID	U.S. Agency for International Development
USITC	U.S. International Trade Commission
USPTO	United States Patent and Trademark Office
USTR	U.S. Trade Representative
WDI	World Development Indicators
WTO	World Trade Organization

Chapter 1. Economics as a Domain of Competition

The most recent U.S. National Security Strategy starts with a fundamental assumption that the United States faces growing political, economic, and military competition around the world.[1] Responding to, shaping, and even leading this competition is based on four pillars, of which the second is firmly economic: "Promote American Prosperity."[2] This includes agendas for the domestic economy, international economic relations, innovation, and energy.

This report discusses economic competition from a number of different perspectives. Different types of economic competition really are distinct in their effects. While some may result in zero-sum outcomes, in which one party gains and the other party loses just as much, others may have positive-sum outcomes, in which both parties may gain from competition. Therefore, the relationship between competition and winning and losing may not be obvious. For example, in international economic relations, trade is generally a positive-sum interaction, and even if the industry of one country shrinks relative to the industry of another, both countries may end up better off, at least in overall economic terms. Another example is policy that aims to develop specific industries, with the intent of establishing a global industry leader. Governments may guess wrong as to which industries will develop or even be important in future years, thus wasting money trying to develop an industry that could be obsolete before it is created.

Although international economic competition—which focuses on trade, investment, and finance relationships—can affect domestic prosperity, domestic economic policy usually has the preponderant effect on domestic prosperity. International competition has little effect on how policymakers may choose their domestic labor regulations or professional licensing regimes, especially if the domestic market is large relative to transactions with the international market. In fact, appeals to international competitiveness have been used in the past to mask poor domestic policy choices.

As will be discussed throughout this report, there is a lack of agreement on what exactly economic competition means. At one extreme, countries do not compete—companies compete. When considered this way, the idea of competition among countries is meaningless. At another extreme, countries vie to control international economic rules, originate and control the most demanded future technologies, increase the market share of the exports of their companies, and

---

[1] The White House, *National Security Strategy of the United States of America*, Washington, D.C., December 2017.

[2] The White House, *National Security Strategy*, p. 17.

attract more international investment, the latter two goals harkening back to the eighteenth-century mercantilism that Adam Smith and David Ricardo opposed.[3]

There is some element of truth in each of these positions, although not in the sense of splitting the difference. Companies compete. A large proportion of world trade occurs within companies and business networks, in global value chains, so that while the profits from exports may accrue to company owners, employment occurs and wages are paid in foreign countries.[4] An example of this is the small print on the back of an Apple iPhone: "Designed by Apple in California. Assembled in China." In these cases, companies are competing, but many of the benefits are accruing to other countries.[5]

Nations compete. Many economists believe that innovation and some level of control of new technologies is fundamental to prosperity.[6] In addition, these technologies can give a defense and security edge. Economic size and dominance in certain sectors may also provide a country leverage over other countries, again for defense and security purposes. The United States has demonstrated this with its central role in the global financial system and therefore the effect of economic sanctions and other tools it imposes.

Accordingly, economic competition can be understood in two ways. The first is competition as outcome. Results are measured by aggregate outcomes, such as per capita gross domestic product (GDP). Better outcomes in one country may have little bearing on outcomes in another, and countries that are not the highest or best in the outcome being measured may still enjoy strong economic performance and good quality of life.

The second is competition as action. The focus is on government policies, programs, or other actions designed to achieve specific results generally focused on a relative economic or even geopolitical gain. Actions may also ultimately lead to positive aggregate outcomes, but the successful pursuit of a relative economic gain can come at an absolute cost. Trade is generally beneficial to all parties participating in it; skewing the competition in one's favor may shift the relative gains but hobble growth in both countries. Sanctions and tariffs are likely to have such an effect. There can thus be a trade-off between maximizing economic outcomes and succeeding

---

[3] Adam Smith, *An Inquiry into the Nature and Causes of the Wealth of Nations*, London: William Strahan and Thomas Cadell, 1776; David Ricardo, *On the Principles of Political Economy and Taxation*, London: John Murray, 1817. Mercantilism is a term used to describe seventeenth- and eighteenth-century writings on trade that encouraged state regulation of trade, protection of domestic sectors, and the fostering of trade surpluses as a means of increasing national wealth, maximizing employment, and increasing the overall power of the state. For a more complete description, see Douglas A. Irwin, *Against the Tide: An Intellectual History of Free Trade*, Princeton, N.J.: Princeton University Press, 1996.

[4] Richard Baldwin, *The Great Convergence: Information Technology and the New Globalization*, Cambridge, Mass.: Belknap Press of Harvard University Press, 2016.

[5] This is not to minimize the benefits of exporting even via global value chains. In the case of Apple, the production arrangements support high-wage employment in the United States.

[6] George Magnus, "Forget Trade Wars, the Real U.S.-China Clash Is a Tech War," *Prospect*, March 26, 2018.

2

at a competitive action. Actions therefore need to take account of not just benefits but costs as well.

Economic competition, however defined, has direct and indirect relevance to the U.S. armed forces. Most important, a wealthy country with a large economy can more easily fund the personnel, equipment, and technology the armed forces use. It can support more innovation and development of new technologies, including commercial technologies that are useful to the armed forces. And the trade and investment orientation of countries could affect their political orientation, influencing alliance and partnership possibilities and future security challenges.

The research for this report was conducted within a broader RAND Corporation project on *America and Strategic Competition in the 21st Century* and was concluded in October 2019. This report first defines competition and highlights overall economic aspects within the context of the Strategic Competition project. It then moves to a discussion of how economists have generally viewed "competitiveness," which is a stand-in for international competition. Next it discusses how countries compete for markets, technologies, and standards, noting differences regarding whether there are first-order effects on prosperity and power or whether these actions are swamped by domestic policies. The report also discusses the use of economic tools in geopolitical and security competition, and competition over setting the overall rules for the international economy, then goes into more depth on why this competition is relevant to the U.S. armed forces. A final section discusses policy implications.

Defining Competition

Competition involves two or more parties contending for some scarce goal with the outcome being that one of the parties will enhance its power or influence relative to another. This does not mean the outcome needs to be zero-sum, but it is also not equally win-win. Based on these characteristics, this report and the project on Strategic Competition have adopted the following broad definition of competition:

> Competition in the international realm involves the attempt to gain advantage, often relative to others believed to pose a challenge or threat, through the self-interested pursuit of contested goods such as power, security, wealth, influence, and status.[7]

Economic competition is perceived to occur in a number of different areas. First, countries may compete for leadership in specific industries.[8] However, the connection between purposeful government policy to create leadership in these industries and actual leadership is not necessarily obvious. Nor is it obvious that leadership, however defined, is desirable, given that the resources used to attain leadership could have been used for other purposes more effectively.

---

[7] Michael J. Mazarr et al., *Understanding the Emerging Era of International Competition: Theoretical and Historical Perspectives*, Santa Monica, Calif.: RAND Corporation, RR-2726-AF, 2018, p. 5.

[8] Mazarr et al., *Understanding the Emerging Era*, p. 5.

Countries may also compete to ensure that other nations or international systems adhere to the instituting nation's preferred norms and rules.[9] This is directly applicable to economics with two fundamental characteristics of nondiscrimination in international trade: the most-favored nation (MFN) clause—insisted on by the United States in the General Agreement on Tariffs and Trade (GATT), the first major post–WWII multilateral trade agreement—and national treatment.[10] In the context of international trade agreements, MFN holds that all partners must receive the same treatment as the best available to any individual partner. National treatment means that foreign goods and services, and subsequent to the original GATT, foreign investment, must receive the same treatment as domestic goods, services, and investment.

In this context, "predatory, regime-destroying trade policies" designed to damage another nation's economy could be a form of economic competition.[11] Likewise, the use of state-owned enterprises or state-guided enterprises in ways that are incompatible with existing norms and rules of international exchange may be a form of economic competition.[12]

Countries may also compete simply to have the highest level of material economic prosperity.[13] Given the outsize role of domestic economic policy in growth and productivity, this type of competition is more akin to bodybuilding than a soccer game (the latter being more like competing to dominate an export market) or a street fight with few rules (using economic tools to undermine another country's economy).

Countries may compete over control of or access to resources, which is another form of economic competition.[14] In fact, natural resources—typically oil—have been a common trigger for interstate wars and militarized border disputes.[15]

Finally, economic competition may involve using economic tools in other forms of competition. In this domain, the most well-known acts include sanctions, particularly comprehensive financial sanctions of the type that brought Iran to negotiations over its nuclear program. Actions could also include cyberattacks on infrastructure and even slowing down or blocking transit of goods over borders, as China has done to Mongolia.

---

[9] Mazarr et al., *Understanding the Emerging Era*, p. 21.

[10] On MFN, see Douglas A. Irwin, "GATT Turns 60," *Wall Street Journal*, April 9, 2007; and Douglas A. Irwin, Petros C. Mavroidis, and Alan O. Sykes, "The Genesis of the GATT," Dartmouth College; Columbia Law School, University of Neuchâtel, and Centre for Economic Policy Research; and Stanford Law School, December 19, 2007. On national treatment, see John H. Jackson, "National Treatment Obligations and Non-Tariff Barriers," *Michigan Journal of International Law*, Vol. 10, No. 1, 1989, pp. 207–224.

[11] Mazarr et al., *Understanding the Emerging Era*, p. 24.

[12] Mazarr et al., *Understanding the Emerging Era*, p. 21.

[13] Mazarr et al., *Understanding the Emerging Era*, p. 21.

[14] Mazarr et al., *Understanding the Emerging Era*, p. 21.

[15] Francesco Caselli, Massimo Morelli, and Dominic Rohner, "The Geography of Interstate Resource Wars," *Quarterly Journal of Economics*, Vol. 130, No. 1, February 2015, pp. 267–315.

As an entrée into economic competition, this report starts with economic outcomes. These outcomes may not be the result of competition but may instead result more from domestic economic policies. Nonetheless, they do show the standings of the United States and its allies in the world economy as of the mid-2010s.

The United States in the Global Economy

Regardless of the view of economic competition, it is useful to understand the United States' place in the global economy. Doing so is a prime example of competition as outcome. Tables 1.1, 1.2, and 1.3 provide key indicators for specific years since 1990 for the four largest economies in

Table 1.1. Domestic Economic Indicators for the World's Leading Economies

Country	1990	2000	2010	2018
Gross domestic product ($B)				
China	361	1,211	6,087	13,608
European Union	7,579	8,910	17,010	18,749
Japan	3,133	4,888	5,700	4,971
United States	5,963	10,252	14,992	20,494
Share of world GDP (%)				
China	2	4	9	16
European Union	34	27	26	22
Japan	14	15	9	6
United States	26	31	23	24
Per capita GDP ($PPP)				
China	1,522	3,690	9,498	16,187
European Union	24,868	30,299	34,135	38,076
Japan	30,582	33,872	35,750	39,294
United States	36,813	45,661	49,479	55,681
Unemployment rate (%)				
China	2.4	3.3	4.5	4.4
European Union	8.6	9.3	9.5	6.8
Japan	2.1	4.7	5.1	2.4
United States	6.8	4.0	9.6	3.9
Youth unemployment rate (%)				
China	4.4	6.9	9.8	10.6
European Union	18.4	19.9	22.1	17.1
Japan	4.5	9.1	9.5	3.7
United States	13.3	9.2	18.3	8.2

SOURCE: World Bank, World Development Indicators (WDI), data downloaded July 18, 2019.
NOTES: Gross domestic product is in billions of nominal dollars and is the WDI variable NY.GDP.MKTP.DC. Share of world GDP is in percentage terms and is nominal GDP for the geographic entity relative to world GDP using the GDP variable NY.GDP.MKTP.DC. Per capita GDP is in terms of purchasing-power parity in constant 2011 international dollars and is WDI variable NY.GDP.PCAP.PP.KD. Unemployment rate listed as 1990 is actually for 1991 and is WDI variable SL.UEM.TOTL.ZS. The youth unemployment rate listed as 1990 is actually for 1991 and is WDI variable SL.UEM.1524.ZS. Youth unemployment is measured for people ages 15 to 24. Both unemployment rates are modeled ILO (International Labour Organization) estimates.

the world, including the three largest single-country economies—the United States, China, and Japan—and the European Union (EU), a unified market of 28 member states at the time of the research but 27 member states as of January 31, 2020.[16]

The United States remains the world's single-largest economy, at least as of 2018, with a GDP valued at $20.5 trillion. GDP is the value of all goods and services produced within a jurisdiction; it is equivalent to the value of all income earned within a jurisdiction. Although China's share of world GDP has been continuously increasing, the U.S. share of the global economy was only slightly smaller in 2018 than it was in 1990, albeit with some volatility. In contrast, the share of the closest U.S. allies—the EU and Japan—has shrunk notably and consistently.

As noted previously, all schools of thought on economic competition agree that a goal is to provide for a high standard of living. This is best measured as per capita GDP in terms of purchasing-power parity (PPP), which takes account of different prices for the same good or service in different economies. For example, a haircut is much cheaper in China than in Germany, but it is still a haircut. If a Chinese resident can afford four haircuts a month but a German resident can afford only one haircut each month, then in some ways, the resident of China is wealthier. In general, nontradable products and services, such as haircuts, have more variation in prices than do tradable products, such as cars or clothing.[17]

China's per capita GDP in PPP terms has grown dramatically since 1990, from about $1,500 to $16,000—an annual growth rate of 8.8 percent. In contrast, per capita GDP in PPP terms grew 1.5 percent annually in the European Union and the United States and 0.9 percent annually in Japan.[18] However, because China started from such a low base, the developed economies of the EU, Japan, and the United States retained far higher standards of living as of 2018, with the United States by far the wealthiest. That year, U.S. per capita GDP in PPP terms was 3.4 times that of China, almost 1.5 times that of the EU, and 1.4 times that of Japan.

Part of having a high standard of living is having a job. China and Japan have exhibited the most stability in unemployment rates, one measure of the health of the labor market. Technically, the unemployment rate is the percentage of people actively looking for work relative to the total number of people either employed or actively looking for work. It does not account for people

---

[16] Boris Johnson (Prime Minister, United Kingdom), *PM Address to the Nation: 31 January 2020*, Prime Minister's Office, 10 Downing Street, January 31, 2020.

[17] PPP rates can also be used for aggregate GDP. However, international trade and investment take place at nominal market exchange rates, and so PPP aggregate GDP does not reflect a country's ability to engage in international exchange. However, PPP rates can be used to compare domestic living standards because they include traded and nontraded goods when purchased within the home country. One flaw of using PPP rates to compare domestic standards of living is that they are based on a common basket of goods and services. However, people in different countries often purchase different baskets of goods and services, sometimes because of price and sometimes because of different preferences.

[18] Specifically, per capita GDP in PPP terms grew 8.81 percent per year in China, 1.53 percent in the EU, 1.49 percent in the United States, and 0.90 in Japan.

not looking for work, either because they are doing home activities, are discouraged, are in school, are elderly, or have other reasons, and it counts as a job both part-time and full-time work. China's state-controlled economy is designed to keep employment stable, although at some cost to efficiency. The Japanese economy has also traditionally featured stable employment arrangements, although in recent years there has been more nonregular employment, such as through fixed-term contracting.[19]

Labor markets in the United States are more volatile. During periods of economic growth, unemployment falls to levels at or below those of Japan and China. But during recessions, unemployment tends to rise. This was especially true of the period 2008 to 2010, during the Great Recession and its immediate aftermath. Europe, in contrast, has consistently high unemployment rates. Labor-market rigidities, such as strong regulations about firing and benefits, and weak economic growth result in less job creation for people who want work.

These patterns repeat for youth unemployment, which is the unemployment rate for people ages 15 to 24. It is higher than overall unemployment rates worldwide, but among major economies it is particularly high in the European Union. Notably, it has been rising in China. This could be a negative signal for the future if it means larger numbers of young people now than in the past are not forming employment skills early in their careers.

All major economies are relatively unequal when it comes to income before taxes and transfers (Table 1.2). Income inequality in many economies worldwide has risen over the past several decades. Both causes and consequences are debated. Causes may include technological change that favors highly educated people; globalization that increases competition among lower-skilled workers worldwide, suppressing wages in wealthier countries because workers in poorer countries can do similar work for a lower wage; or even greater use of laws and regulations by influential social groups to favor themselves. Consequences may be public perceptions of systemic unfairness—leading voters to support political leaders who promise to make things more fair (whether they can actually do so or not)—slower economic growth, and less intergenerational mobility. But the promise of high economic rewards might also spur innovation that broadly raises living standards, although at different rates for different groups. Furthermore, policies for moderating inequality while retaining incentives for innovation and growth remain debated as well.[20]

---

[19] Koji Takahashi, "The Future of the Japanese Style Employment System: Continued Long-Term Employment and the Challenges It Faces," *Japan Labor Issues*, Vol. 2, No. 6, April–May 2018, pp. 6–15.

[20] Era Dabla-Norris et al., *Causes and Consequences of Income Inequality: A Global Perspective*, IMF Staff Discussion Note, International Monetary Fund, SDN/15/13, June 2015; N. Gregory Mankiw, "Defending the 1 Percent," *Journal of Economic Perspectives*, Vol. 27, No. 3, Summer 2013, pp. 21–34; Miles Corak, "Income Inequality, Equality of Opportunity, and Intergenerational Mobility," *Journal of Economic Perspectives*, Vol. 27, No. 3, Summer 2013, pp. 79–102.

Table 1.2. Income Inequality in the World's Leading Economies

Country	1995	2000	2005	2010	2015
Gini coefficient, pretax and transfer					
China	—	—	—	0.548	—
European Union	0.472	0.480	0.495	0.496	0.503
Japan	0.403	0.432	0.462	0.488	0.504
United States	0.477	.0476	0.486	0.499	0.506
Gini coefficient, posttax and transfer					
China	—	—	—	0.514	—
European Union	0.299	0.300	0.311	0.309	0.312
Japan	0.323	0.337	0.329	0.336	0.339
United States	0.361	0.357	.0380	0.38	0.390

SOURCES: Organisation for Economic Co-Operation and Development, "Income Distribution Database (IDD)," 2018a, data downloaded July 18, 2019 and July 19, 2019; United Nations, World Population Prospects, 2019b, data query, data downloaded July 18, 2019.

NOTES: Gini coefficients are a measure of inequality and range from 0 (total equality) to 1 (all income is held by one person) and are from the OECD. Variables are "Gini (market income, before taxes and transfers)" and "Gini (disposable income, post taxes and transfers)." Coefficients were computed based on an income definition until 2011 and a new income definition since 2012. Whenever available, the coefficients based on the new income definition were used, but when those were unavailable, coefficients based on the old income definition were used. Totals for the European Union are population-weighted averages since there was no EU-wide variable. For 1995, the following countries were used for the pretax coefficient: Czech Republic, Denmark, Finland, France, Germany, Italy, Netherlands, Sweden, and United Kingdom. The following countries were used for the posttax coefficient: Denmark, Finland, Germany, Greece, Hungary, Italy, Luxembourg, Netherlands, Sweden, and United Kingdom. For 2000, the following countries were used for both coefficients: Denmark, Finland, France, Germany, Italy, Netherlands, Sweden, and United Kingdom. The following additional countries were used for the posttax coefficient: Greece, Hungary, and Luxembourg. For 2005, the following countries were used for both coefficients: Belgium, Czech Republic, Denmark, Estonia, Finland, France, Germany, Greece, Ireland, Italy, Latvia, Lithuania, Luxembourg, Netherlands, Poland, Portugal, Slovak Republic, Slovenia, Sweden, and United Kingdom. The following additional country was used for the posttax coefficient: Hungary. For both 2010 and 2015, 23 of the 28 current EU countries were included: Austria, Belgium, Czech Republic, Denmark, Estonia, Finland, France, Germany, Greece, Hungary, Ireland, Italy, Latvia, Lithuania, Luxembourg, Netherlands, Poland, Portugal, Slovak Republic, Slovenia, Spain, Sweden, and the United Kingdom. In some cases, adjacent years were used. For pretax, they included China (2011 for 2010); Czech Republic (1996 for 1995); France (1996 for 1995); Germany (2004 for 2005); Hungary (2009 for 2010 and 2014 for 2015); Italy (2004 for 2005); Japan (2006 for 2005 and 2009 for 2010); Sweden (2004 for 2005); and the United Kingdom (1994 for 1995). For posttax, they included China (2011 for 2010); Greece (1994 for 1995 and 1999 for 2000); Hungary (2009 for 2010 and 2014 for 2015); Japan (2006 for 2005 and 2009 for 2010); Luxembourg (1996 for 1995 and 2001 for 2000); Sweden (2004 for 2005); and the United Kingdom (1994 for 1995).

The Gini coefficient, a measure of inequality, ranges from 0 (most equal) to 1 (most unequal). Before taxes and transfers, the United States and the European Union are actually quite similar. Japan, based on available data, is relatively more equal in its income distribution.

Major differences arise after taxes and transfers. Similar to the labor-market protections it has instituted, the European Union is also the most aggressive major economy regarding redistribution. Japan also actively redistributes income, as does the United States, although to a lesser degree. In contrast, China, even after taxes and transfers, is highly unequal—even more so than the other major economies *before* taxes and transfers.

Other aspects of domestic economic performance are not as easily captured. For example, most major economies have high and rising levels of debt. Among the advanced economies—

some countries of the European Union, Japan, and the United States—the value of this debt is known and is largely recognized as an important economic issue, although repaying it could be a challenge. If it continues to mount, it could have negative effects on growth and the government's ability to continue funding some programs. In China, high levels of debt are less transparent and have led to warnings from such organizations as the International Monetary Fund (IMF). There, the issue is not only growth effects but also uncertainties about how the government will respond in the event of debt problems.

In sum, the major advanced economies—the European Union, Japan, and the United States— all provide decent economic performance to benefit their populations in terms of per capita income and the after-tax distribution of income. Europe faces ongoing challenges regarding the creation of jobs for people who want them. China has grown dramatically, and hundreds of millions of people are enjoying standards of living that their grandparents would have never imagined. However, as reflected in the Gini coefficient, this prosperity is not shared throughout the society, and China still has hundreds of millions of people, perhaps a third of the population or more, with very poor standards of living.

In sum, given China's starting point, it appears that all major economies are fulfilling the basic goals of economic competitiveness—providing a decent standard of living, or the hope of one in the future—to the vast majority of their populations.

The measures discussed so far may benefit from global engagement but are not direct measures of international competition, either by companies or countries. For that, we now turn to trade and foreign direct investment, or cross-border investment with the purpose of controlling a business (Table 1.3).

The United States is by far the largest trading economy among single countries and has been so for decades. The 28 member countries of the EU constitute the largest unified trading economy. In part, this is because trade among EU members—such as German exports to Italy, and French exports to Poland—are counted as international trade. However, even excluding this intra-EU trade, the EU is the largest trader and the largest exporter. Certainly, one reason the United States is the largest single-nation trading economy is because it is also the largest importer and runs a substantial trade deficit. However, it is also a substantial exporter.

Although the United States is the largest single-nation trading economy, it is far less dependent on trade than the other countries, with trade amounting to only 27 percent of U.S. GDP in 2018. In all four major economies, trade relative to GDP was far higher in 2010 than in 1990, but in the United States and China it has since receded. As of 2018, when considering only extra-EU trade, China's, the European Union's, and Japan's trade dependence were all similar, at 38 percent, 35 percent, and 37 percent, respectively. This suggests they are all more vulnerable to international economic turbulence than the United States would be.

These major economies are intertwined. In 2017, Japan sent 49 percent of its goods exports to the other three major economies. For China, this figure was 42 percent; for the EU it was

Table 1.3. International Economic Indicators for the World's Leading Economies

Country	1990	2000	2010	2018[a]
Total trade ($B)				
China	104	351	2,985	5,199
European Union	3,931	5,967	12,898	16,744
European Union—extra-EU	—	2,225	5,113	6,601
Japan	616	978	1,662	1,855
United States	1,151	2,523	4,201	5,624
Total trade relative to GDP (%)				
China	29	29	49	38
European Union	52	67	76	89
European Union—extra-EU	—	25	30	35
Japan	20	20	29	37
United States	19	25	28	27
Exports of goods and services ($B)				
China	57	190	1,604	2,651
European Union	1,982	2,989	6,532	8,662
European Union—extra-EU	—	1,074	2,550	3,452
Japan	320	524	870	929
United States	535	1,075	1,853	2,501
Imports of goods and services ($B)				
China	47	161	1,381	2,548
European Union	1,950	2,979	6,367	8,082
European Union—extra-EU	—	1,152	2,563	3,149
Japan	296	455	792	925
United States	616	1,448	2,348	3,123
Outward FDI stock ($B)				
China	4	28	317	1,482
European Union	976	2,907	9,137	10,632
European Union—extra-EU	—	—	5,595	8,376
Japan	201	278	831	1,520
United States	732	2,694	4,810	7,799
Inward FDI stock ($B)				
China	21	193	588	1,491
European Union	884	2,322	7,357	9,124
European Union—extra-EU	—	—	4,171	7,114
Japan	10	50	215	207
United States	540	2,783	3,422	7,807

SOURCES: World Bank, World Development Indicators (WDI), data downloaded July 18, 2019; Eurostat, "European Union Balance of Payments—Quarterly Data (BPM6) [bop_eu6_qt]," 2019, data downloaded July 18, 2019; Eurostat, "Archive: Foreign Direct Investment Statistics," Statistics Explained, March 19, 2018; Eurostat, "The Net Investment Position of the EU down at €1, 100 Billion," news release 200/2018, December 20, 2018; United Nations Conference on Trade and Development, UNCTADStat, data downloaded July 18, 2019; Board of Governors of the Federal Reserve, U.S./Euro Foreign Exchange Rate (DEXUSEU), undated, data downloaded July 18, 2019.

NOTES: All data are in billions of nominal dollars. The following applies to all variables except the extra-EU European Union trade in 2000, 2010, and 2018 and the extra-EU European Union FDI in 2010 and 2017. Total trade is exports of goods and services plus imports of goods and services on a balance of payments (BOP) basis except for Japan in 1990, which is on a non-BOP basis; exports of goods and services is WDI variable BX.GSR.GNFS.CD except for Japan in 1990, which is WDI variable NE.EXP.GNFS.CD; imports of goods and services is WDI variable BM.GSR.GNFS.CD except for Japan in 1990, which is WDI variable NE.IMP.GNFS.CD. FDI data from UNCTADStat were not available for 2018. The variable trade relative to GDP is trade, as described above, relative to GDP for the geographic entity using GDP variable NY.GDP.MKTP.DC.

Extra-EU trade for the European Union in 2000, 2010, and 2018 is from Eurostat and is specifically for goods and services credits and debits as recorded in "European Union Balance of Payments—Quarterly Data." Values for extra-EU trade and FDI were in euros and were converted to dollars using annual exchange rates from the Board of Governors of the Federal Reserve System via FRED.

[a] 2017 for FDI.

33 percent, and for the United States it was 31 percent.[21] For goods imports, the figures for China, the EU, Japan, and the United States were 31 percent, 38 percent, 47 percent, and 46 percent, respectively.

As high-income economies, the EU and especially the United States specialize in services exports, so their trade exposure is even higher than indicated by the goods exports figures. For example, in 2017, the United States sent 35 percent of its goods *and* services exports to the three major economies, compared to 31 percent of goods exports.[22] But it received 46 percent of its goods *and* services exports from those economies, the same share as its goods exports.

Finally, consider FDI, which is cross-border investment aimed at controlling a business. The United States is the single-largest investor among individual countries. The U.S. lead means that U.S. companies—not the United States as a country—own a larger share of foreign businesses than do companies from other countries. In the reverse direction, the United States is also the largest site of inward FDI. As with trade, FDI is intertwined among the major advanced economies.

The European Union is also a major investor. As with trade, FDI within the European Union is considered international. Considering just FDI from the European Union to countries outside the EU, the European Union is a larger investing entity than is the United States. Considering just FDI from countries outside the EU to the EU, the United States remains a larger host of investment by multinationals.

Numerous other international economic indicators are relevant but are not included in Table 1.3. One is a financial measure. The U.S. dollar constitutes the majority currency in international reserves—foreign currencies held by other countries—and is the dominant currency used in international trade transactions. The international use of the dollar has allowed the United States to borrow more easily and to exercise leverage with financial sanctions when it sees fit to do so.

In sum, the United States is still the world's leading economy on a number of dimensions of international transactions. It is the largest single-nation trader, the largest single-nation investor, and the dominant financial hub in the world. This certainly contributes to aggregate domestic economic prosperity. The open question is how it translates into international power.

---

[21] United Nations, UN Comtrade Database, 2019a. The data were downloaded July 24, 2019. Reexports and reimports are excluded from these calculations.

[22] U.S. Bureau of Economic Analysis, "U.S. Trade in Goods and Services by Selected Countries and Areas, 1999–Present," Excel spreadsheet, last updated June 19, 2019. Another 26 percent of exports went to Canada and Mexico, and 24 percent were received from Canada and Mexico.

Chapter 2. Strategic Competition in Economics

Economists have long debated exactly what is meant by competitiveness. The issue enters into the realm of strategic competition among nations because one view holds that competitiveness relates to the global market position of a national industry. In the United States in the late 1980s and early 1990s, this pertained largely to the global position of high-technology industries.

For example, in 1990, the Senate Finance Committee asked the U.S. International Trade Commission (USITC) to study the global competitiveness of the U.S. telecommunications, semiconductor manufacturing and testing equipment, and pharmaceuticals industries. Furthermore, the reports were to include information on foreign-government policies to make their own industries globally competitive, existing or proposed U.S. government policies to keep or make American industries globally competitive, and impediments in the U.S. economy that might inhibit competitiveness.[1] The USITC defined competitiveness to mean the ability of a company or industry "to sustain relative global market position (sales volume and market share) and profit performance in the context of rapidly changing technology and markets."[2]

The United States was not the only economy concerned with global competitiveness. In what was then the European Community, a landmark European Commission white paper noted that for employment prospects in the European Union to improve, the global competitiveness of European industries must improve. It called for national and European Community authorities not only to provide a favorable environment for business, but to promote international competitiveness.[3]

In many cases, those writing about the need to pay attention to international competitiveness said that domestic economic policies were the most important element in national economic well-being. For example, one noted author wrote, "Flawed domestic choices, not unfair foreign trading practices, are the main cause of the nation's long-run economic slowdown."[4] Another wrote, "Ninety-three percent of economic success or failure is determined at home with only

---

[1] U.S. International Trade Commission, *Global Competitiveness of U.S. Advanced-Technology Manufacturing Industries: Semiconductor Manufacturing and Testing Equipment*, Report to the Committee on Finance, United States Senate, on Investigation No. 332-303 Under Section 332(g) of the Tariff Act of 1930, USITC Publication 2434, September 1991.

[2] U.S. International Trade Commission, *Global Competitiveness*, p. 1-1.

[3] European Commission, *Growth, Competitiveness, Employment: That Challenges and Way Forward into the 21st Century: White Paper*, Luxembourg: Office for Official Publications of the European Communities, 1994.

[4] Laura D'Andrea Tyson, *Who's Bashing Whom? Trade Conflict in High-Technology Industries*, Washington, D.C.: Institute for International Economics, November 1992, p. 2.

seven percent depending on competitive and cooperative arrangements with the rest of the world."[5]

However, behind the competitiveness arguments were a variety of propositions: A nation benefited from success in high-technology industries, with those benefits including higher productivity and correspondingly high-wage jobs. Meeting the test of international markets was essential to the success of these industries. Furthermore, there was significant government involvement in trade in the products of those industries worldwide; therefore, traditional trade policies were no longer helping produce prosperity. As a result, governments needed to design policies to help those industries sell into foreign markets.[6] For the European Community, the policy response was to also include finding a new balance between competition and cooperation, including carefully fostering strategic alliances to allow European firms to counterbalance their U.S. and Japanese competitors.[7]

This focus on competitiveness reached its 1990s peak with a debate sparked by Paul Krugman in a *Foreign Affairs* article called "Competitiveness: A Dangerous Obsession."[8] He wrote that the idea that a country's economic success is determined by how well it performs in world markets is "flatly wrong. That is, it is simply not the case that the world's leading nations are to any important degree in economic competition with each other, or that any of their major economic problems can be attributed to failures to compete on world markets."[9] Among other issues he raised were the fact that a trade deficit can be a sign of economic strength, that countries are not corporations, that trade can be mutually beneficial—so that simply having a larger market share is not necessarily a sign of success—and that, most important, it is domestic productivity that determines domestic standards of living, and this is only loosely connected to performance on world markets.

The reaction was swift from those arguing that international competition and industrial policy were important. In essence, the argument was that advanced technology sectors are the source of well-paying jobs and productivity increases, that the United States should introduce policies to foster those sectors, and that ensuring that America does have strong, internationally competitive technology sectors will strengthen growth prospects.[10]

---

[5] Lester Thurow, "Microchips, Not Potato Chips," *Foreign Affairs*, July/August 1994.

[6] Tyson, *Who's Bashing Whom?*; Thurow, "Microchips, Not Potato Chips."

[7] European Commission, *Growth, Competitiveness, Employment*, pp. 75–76.

[8] Paul Krugman, "Competitiveness: A Dangerous Obsession," *Foreign Affairs*, March/April 1994, pp. 28–44.

[9] Krugman, "Competitiveness," p. 30.

[10] Thurow, "Microchips, Not Potato Chips." In his *Foreign Affairs* article, Thurow referred to the competitiveness and industrial policy advocates as "the gang of eight" and mentioned President Bill Clinton, British Prime Minister John Major, European Commission President Jacques Delors, Clinton Secretary of Labor Robert Reich, Clinton Council of Economic Advisers Chair Laura D'Andrea Tyson, Clinton U.S. Trade Representative Mickey Kantor, Clinton Health Care Task Force head Ira Magaziner, and himself.

The argument about the need for industrial policy and national coordination died out for a time, in particular during the rapid development of the internet and telecommunications sectors, which suddenly seemed to emerge and succeed internationally without coordinated government policy. But it has never gone away. Notably, the government was involved in the development of the internet, but not with the goal of having it develop the way it did. The Advanced Research Projects Agency (ARPA), now the Defense Advanced Research Projects Agency (DARPA), demonstrated the ARPANET network in 1969,[11] and in 1973, initiated a research program to enable computer networks to communicate across what were known as packet networks.[12] This program resulted in the Transmission Control Protocol and Internet Protocol, or TCP/IP Protocol Suite. In 1986, the National Science Foundation initiated the NSFNET, now an important internet backbone communication service. Civilian industry eventually became involved and the internet took off as a public resource. In the absence of some initial government funding, the internet may not have developed the way that it did and the United States might not be the dominant player in information technology.

However, even successfully targeting a sector and succeeding at creating it might not have an appreciable effect on an economy. The creation and support of the aviation company Embraer in Brazil is a good illustration: Created in 1969, Embraer was the world's largest producer of regional jets in 2018.[13] And Brazil certainly has grown, but out of 97 countries with available data, its growth of per capita GDP between 1969 and 2016 was ranked 37, behind less technology-focused Latin American and Caribbean countries such as Dominican Republic, Panama, Chile, Paraguay, Colombia, Costa Rica, and Uruguay. Furthermore, Brazilian growth has largely leveled off—per capital GDP in real terms in 2010 U.S. dollars was $10,244 in 2007 and $10,869 in 2016.[14] Brazil created a technologically advanced, globally competitive company, but it remains an open question as to whether those resources might have been better used for measures that might have had a broader-based effect.

For most economists, competitiveness is now taken to mean a focus on domestic economic policies in support of the ability to spur increases in productivity and standards of living. For example, one set of authors described competitiveness as based on three sets of policies: social infrastructure and political institutions, monetary and fiscal policy, and national business environment.[15] Likewise, the World Economic Forum, which produces the *Global Competitiveness Report*, defines competitiveness as the "*set of institutions, policies, and factors that determine*

---

[11] Defense Advanced Research Projects Agency, "About Us: ARPANET," webpage, undated.

[12] The information about the development of the TCP/IP Protocol Suite and the NSFNET is from Vint Cerf, "A Brief History of the Internet and Related Networks," Internet Society, undated.

[13] Joe Leahy, Peggy Hollinger, and Patti Waldmeir, "Boeing Strikes Deal for Control of Embraer Regional Jet Operations," *Financial Times*, July 5, 2018.

[14] World Bank, World Development Indicators, 2019, variable NY.GDP.PCAP.KD.

[15] Mercedes Delgado et al., "The Determinants of National Competitiveness," Working Paper 18249, National Bureau of Economic Research, July 2012.

the level of productivity of an economy, which in turn sets the level of prosperity that the economy can achieve."[16]

Despite that convergence, disagreements remain, largely focusing on which institutions, policies, and factors governments should support. At one end of the range are spending and programs that are unrelated to specific industries or technologies, such as infrastructure and education. Framed this way, achieving competitiveness is closer to competition as outcome rather than competition as objective. There are actions, but they are broadly aimed and intended to improve aggregate outcomes. At the other end of the range, the choice of institutions, policies, and factors may include spending and programs that are more targeted toward specific industries or technologies. Framed this way, achieving competitiveness is closer to competition as action.

One new test case is the rise of China. Although there remains little evidence of economists saying countries compete, some have said that the United States and other countries are right to confront China's policies and even to counter its economic dominance.[17] This point of view is discussed further below.

In addition, the gulf between economists on the one hand and technologists and analysts of geopolitics on the other appears to be incompletely bridged. For example, in 2011, Krugman once again criticized the focus among policymakers on competitiveness, noting that countries are not like corporations, competing in the global marketplace, but advocating broad-based efforts on education and spending to improve national productivity.[18] And, as in 1994, the response by others to this argument was that actually countries compete to take global leadership in technology sectors, and that they should do so to maintain national economic performance.[19] Whether and how much governments *should* support industries in their nations to compete to host technology sectors that dominate global markets is a matter of debate. What is clear, however, is that they do compete to do so, as discussed next.

---

[16] Klaus Schwab, ed., *The Global Competitiveness Report 2017–2018*, Insight Report, Geneva: World Economic Forum, 2017.

[17] Jim Tankersley, "Economists Say U.S. Tariffs Are Wrong Move on a Valid Issue," *New York Times*, April 11, 2018; Arvind Subramanian, "Countering China's Economic Dominance," *Business Standard*, January 20, 2013.

[18] Paul Krugman, "The Competition Myth," *New York Times*, January 23, 2011.

[19] Stephen Ezell, "Krugman Flat Wrong That Competitiveness Is a Myth," Information Technology and Innovation Foundation, January 25, 2011.

Chapter 3. Economic Competition Beyond Competitiveness

Countries conduct economic competition in a number of different ways. They compete for export markets and inward FDI, echoing seventeenth- and eighteenth-century mercantilism. They compete to develop leadership in technology-intensive industries. They also compete to make sure standards that are favorable to their industries are adopted more widely. These domains of competition fall under competition as action.

Competing for Markets and Money

Nearly all countries compete for export markets and inward FDI. Competition for export markets can come in several forms, including some type of subsidized finance, direct help by government officials, and state-owned enterprises competing in markets.

In the realm of export finance, countries often have established institutions. Every single member of the Organisation for Economic Co-operation and Development has such an institution.[1] In the United States, that institution is the Export-Import Bank of the United States; in Korea, it is the Korea Trade Insurance Corporation; in Belgium, it is Credendo.

Such organizations do not exist only in the advanced countries. The most well-known trade finance organization from the developing world is the Export-Import Bank of China, and it illustrates the way countries compete aggressively to open and expand export markets.

Founded in 1994, the China Export-Import Bank operates directly under the leadership of the State Council with the mission to "facilitate national development strategies" and provide financing for "foreign trade, cross-border investment, the Belt and Road Initiative, international industrial capacity and equipment manufacturing cooperation, science and technology, cultural industry, 'going global' endeavors of small and medium enterprises, and the building of an open economy."[2] Certainly, the loans from the bank have the potential to help recipients, although they also help Chinese companies, which tend to get hired for bank-funded projects and use Chinese labor. However, the bank's activities, in particular subsidized finance, can make it far more difficult for companies operating solely with market-based finance to sell to export markets or win construction contracts (with construction as a form of services export) and could provide China leverage over host governments. In addition, the portfolio of the bank tends to be far less transparent than that of Western export finance agencies.[3]

---

[1] Organisation for Economic Co-operation and Development, "Official Export Credit Agencies," webpage, March 7, 2017.

[2] Export-Import Bank of China, "About the Bank: Brief Introduction," webpage, undated.

[3] Todd Moss and Sarah Rose, "China ExIm Bank and Africa: New Lending, New Challenges," CGD Notes, Center for Global Development, November 2006.

Countries also provide direct advice to exporters. For example, the U.S. Commercial Service, part of the U.S. Department of Commerce, provides customized export assistance, including promotional events, trade show representation, and trade missions.[4] Likewise, Austrade, the Australia Trade and Investment Commission, offers tailored services to Australians aiming to export to growing markets, largely in the developing world.[5]

Related to export promotion, countries try to promote their companies to work on major construction and infrastructure projects. In China, the Export-Import Bank plays that role to a large degree. In the United States, not only does the U.S. Commercial Service help with that but a different agency, the Trade and Development Agency, focuses on the range of goods and services U.S. companies can supply to development projects in emerging economies. The agency particularly targets the energy, transportation, and telecommunications sectors.[6]

Notably, despite well-known benefits of imports, countries do not publicly vie for imports. However, trade policymakers recognize the benefits and will use opportunities to lower trade barriers as a way to make their country a more inviting global market destination.

Just as countries try to promote exports in a perceived zero-sum competition, they also try to attract investment from abroad. Singapore pioneered the aggressive pursuit of FDI for development purposes and economic growth (although it certainly did not pioneer the search for foreign investment). At the time of Singapore's independence, in 1965, most developing countries were following a development strategy of import-substituting industrialization by building up local industrial capacity to serve the local market. Shortly after independence, Singapore was one of the few countries to reject this policy and instead turn toward export-led industrialization and the attraction of subsidiaries of multinational corporations.[7] The result has been spectacular, with Singapore per capita GDP in 2010 dollars growing from the equivalent of $3,900 in 1965 to slightly above $52,000 in 2015, a compound rate of 5.3 percent a year, the fourth fastest-growing country during that period. For comparison, U.S. per capita GDP in 2010 dollars in 2015 was slightly below $52,000.[8]

Based in part on the success of Singapore and other rapidly growing Asian economies, China embarked on its reform in the late 1970s and started seeking foreign investment. It established four special economic zones to attract FDI, expand exports, and bring in new technology.[9] Although not the whole story, investment attraction certainly contributed to China growing even

---

[4] Export.gov, "U.S. Commercial Service User Fees," U.S. Department of Commerce, webpage, February 2, 2018.

[5] Austrade.gov, "For Australians: How Austrade Can Help Your Business," Australia Trade and Investment Commission, 2018.

[6] U.S. Trade and Development Agency, "Our Mission," webpage, undated.

[7] Ravi Menon (Managing Director, Monetary Authority of Singapore), "An Economic History of Singapore: 1965–2065," keynote address at the Singapore Economic Review Conference 2015, August 5, 2015.

[8] World Bank, World Development Indicators, online database, version updated July 10, 2019.

[9] Yue-man Yeung, Joanna Lee, and Gordon Kee, "China's Special Economic Zones at 30," *Eurasian Geography and Economics*, Vol. 50, No. 2, 2009, pp. 222–240.

faster than Singapore after 1965, albeit from a very low base, with nearly all of China's growth occurring after 1980. Of all countries with available data, China grew the fastest in terms of per capita GDP from 1980 through 2016, with per capita GDP in 2010 dollars of $187 in 1965 and $6,500 in 2015.

The competition for FDI is now ferocious with not only countries but subnational regions vying for foreign investment. One of the leading trade magazines aimed at helping investors recognizes top national and subnational investment promotion agencies based on responsiveness to inquiries, knowledge and language diversity, databases of sites and incentives, information on permitting and processes, access to recent investors, protection of investor confidentiality, after-investment service, and website.[10] In 2016, the top national agencies were those from Slovenia, Turkey, Korea, Malaysia, Costa Rica, Nicaragua, Ireland, Portugal, Morocco, and South Africa. The best subnational agencies did not necessarily come from the countries with the best national agencies. They included the agencies of Izmir, Turkey; the Aegean Free Zone in Izmir; Hong Kong; Shanghai; the Panama Pacific Special Economic Area; Bogota, Colombia; Saxony-Anhalt, Germany; Copenhagen; Dubai; and Sharjah, United Arab Emirates.

The Innovation Race

Exports and FDI are measurable, and so the competition is easy to watch, which makes it relatively easy to see on a transaction-by-transaction basis which countries are doing best. However, these efforts may not always make an appreciable difference to aggregate economic performance for most countries. Size of economies and distance to markets are the two variables with the strongest relationship to size of trade and investment flows, and all the export and investment promotion in the world cannot change distance and, except in rare instances, do not have large effects on overall size of the economy.

A less measurable area in which nations compete is the development and domination of new technologies. Certainly, ex post, it is possible to see which countries host the dominant firms in a technology area and where the most technologically advanced products come from. But even more than with exports or investment, tracing the pathway from government action to technological dominance is difficult.

The United States has led in technology and innovative industries for decades. Examples include the creation of the internet, the tablet computer, and the smartphone, as well as various web-based services and companies such as Amazon, Facebook, Google, and Twitter. Although China has Alibaba and Taobao in lieu of Amazon, Russia has VKontakte in lieu of or in addition to Facebook, China has Baidu in lieu of Google, and China has Weibo in lieu of Twitter, these are normally described as foreign versions of the U.S. company; the U.S. company is almost never described as the U.S. version of the foreign company. Furthermore, use of the non-U.S.

---

[10] Adam Jones-Kelley, "Top Investment Promotion Agencies," *Site Selection Magazine*, May 2016.

versions is generally limited to a country or a region; the U.S. company or service has worldwide use when it is not blocked by a government.

Technology competition was at the root of the original wave of the competitiveness debate, and it has reemerged, particularly with China's rise. China has become strong in a variety of areas of innovation, science, and technology, and at least some analysts believe it will rival if not surpass the United States.[11]

Some of this increase in innovation capacity can be seen in counts of patents granted (Figure 3.1). From only 42 patents granted to Chinese nationals in 1985 (not shown), the total in 2017 was almost 353,000, placing China as the leading patenting country. China took the lead in 2015, when it passed Japan.

Figure 3.1. Total Patent Grants

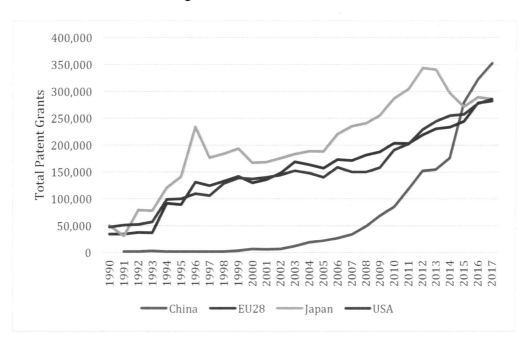

SOURCE: World Intellectual Property Organization, "WIPO Statistics Database," last updated December 2018.
NOTE: Variable is "Total Patent Grants," direct and patent cooperation treaty (PCT) national phase entries.

However, many of these patents were granted in China, and Chinese patent standards are considered to be lower than standards elsewhere.[12] Accordingly, another way to evaluate Chinese patents is to consider triadic patent families, which can be taken to be a measure of high-quality

---

[11] Hal Sirkin, Justin Rose, and Rahul Choraria, "An Innovation-Led Boost for U.S. Manufacturing," Boston Consulting Group, April 17, 2017; Reinhilde Veugelers, "The Challenge of China's Rise as a Science and Technology Powerhouse," *Brink Asia*, August 28, 2017; Briony Harris, "China Is an Innovation Superpower. This Is Why," *World Economic Forum*, February 7, 2018; Dan Wang, "Why China Will Rival the U.S. in High Tech," Bloomberg Opinion, April 25, 2019.

[12] Cheryl Long and Jun Wang, "China's Patent Promotion Policies and Its Quality Implications," Xiamen University and Colgate University, January 20, 2017.

patents. According to the OECD, "Triadic patent families are a set of patents filed at three of these major patent offices: the European Patent Office (EPO), the Japan Patent Office (JPO) and the United States Patent and Trademark Office (USPTO). Triadic patent family counts are attributed to the country of residence of the inventor and to the date when the patent was first registered."[13] Analysts of patents generally consider filings in multiple offices as a sign of quality.[14]

By this measure, Chinese quality patent activity is still much lower than that of the patent leaders, Japan, the United States, and the European Union (Figure 3.2). However, Chinese

Figure 3.2. Triadic Patent Families

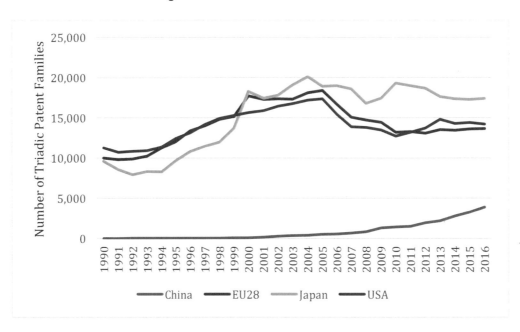

SOURCE: Organisation for Economic Co-operation and Development, "Triadic Patent Families," webpage and database, 2019.
NOTES: According to the OECD, "Triadic patent families are a set of patents filed at three of these major patent offices: the European Patent Office (EPO), the Japan Patent Office (JPO) and the United States Patent and Trademark Office (USPTO). Triadic patent family counts are attributed to the country of residence of the inventor and to the date when the patent was first registered" (OECD, 2018). Triadic patent families can be taken to be a measure of high-quality patents.

---

[13] Organisation for Economic Co-operation and Development, "Triadic Patent Families," webpage and database, 2019.

[14] David Popp, "Using the Triadic Patent Family Database to Study Environmental Innovation," Organisation for Economic Co-operation and Development, 2007; Jay Shambaugh, Ryan Nunn, and Becca Portman, "Eleven Facts About Innovation and Patents," Economic Facts, The Hamilton Project, Brookings Institution, December 2017. Note that multiple filings do not always mean high quality. Research on the quality of patents filed under the patent cooperation treaty (PCT), another form of international patenting, found that while Chinese-origin PCT patents have risen, they are of lower quality than patents from other countries, and the quality has been decreasing (Philipp Boeing and Elisabeth Mueller, "Measuring Patent Quality in International Comparison—Index Development and Application to China," Discussion Paper No. 15-051, ZEW: Zentrum für Europäische Wirtschaftsforschung GmbH, Centre for European Economic Research, July 2015).

innovators are catching up to other major patenting countries. From less than 100 such patents each year between 1985 and 2000, Chinese triadic patent families rose to 3,890 in 2016, but still well below the European Union (13,660), the United States (14,221), and Japan (17,391).

All major economies appear to try to boost their technology industries globally. In the European Union, such sentiments can be found in the 2017 industrial policy strategy.[15] Much of the document focuses on strengthening industry within the European Union. But the policy document also discusses making the EU the global leader in such industries as "next-generation digital technologies"; gaining "a first-mover advantage and global competitive edge" by quickly adopting fifth-generation (5G) connectivity; and maintaining leadership in "green production and clean energy technologies."[16] Global market share is noted, with Europe having world market share of 33 percent in robotics and 55 percent in automotive semiconductors, among other industries.[17] A separate, earlier space strategy document aims to "promote Europe's global leadership in space and increase its share on world space markets."[18] As for exactly what leadership means, European Commission President Jean-Claude Juncker was quite clear in his 2017 State of the Union address: the industrial policy strategy is meant to help EU industries stay or become "number one in innovation, digitisation and decarbonization."[19]

In the United States most recently, this concern about competition for technology industries manifested itself in the President's Council of Advisors on Science and Technology (PCAST) during the administration of President Barack Obama. The council dealt with a variety of issues, many of which did not relate to the economy.[20] However, it also considered how to maintain or establish U.S. global leadership in select industries.

For example, in 2011, the council issued a report aimed at ensuring U.S. leadership in advanced manufacturing.[21] The report argued against an industrial policy supporting specific companies or sectors but instead advocated a more general innovation policy. However, the report did recommend supporting specific technologies, such as by coinvesting in public-private partnerships to help the development of "broadly applicable technologies with transformative potential."[22]

---

[15] European Commission, *Investing in a Smart, Innovative and Sustainable Industry: A Renewed EU Industrial Policy Strategy*, COM(2017) 479 Final, Brussels, September 13, 2017.

[16] European Commission, *Investing*, p. 9.

[17] European Commission, *Investing*, p. 8.

[18] As cited in European Commission, *Investing*, p. 5.

[19] Jean-Claude Juncker, "President Jean-Claude Juncker's State of the Union Address 2017," Brussels, September 13, 2017.

[20] Office of Science and Technology Policy, "PCAST Documents and Reports," webpage, 2017.

[21] President's Council of Advisors on Science and Technology, *Report to the President on Ensuring American Leadership in Advanced Manufacturing*, Executive Office of the President, June 2011.

[22] President's Council of Advisors on Science and Technology, *Report to the President on Ensuring American Leadership in Advanced Manufacturing*, p. 23.

One of PCAST's last reports was aimed at ensuring American leadership in semiconductors.[23] The report noted that progress in semiconductors has fostered new industries and benefited the U.S. and global economies. It also noted that semiconductors were critical to U.S. defense and that cybersecurity relied on the integrity of this technology. But one of the chief motivators for concentrating on U.S. leadership in semiconductors was competition from another country, particularly the way that country was competing: "… Chinese industrial policies aimed at achieving a global leadership position in semiconductor design and manufacturing through nonmarket means, together with the steady growth in Chinese domestic semiconductor consumption, are now compounding those challenges."[24] Although again not recommending a detailed industrial policy, the report did advocate that the U.S. government develop and execute a strategy to both sustain U.S. leadership and drive innovation and specifically to select challenges for innovation on which government, industry, and academia can collaborate.[25]

The administration of President Donald Trump has continued efforts to maintain and expand U.S. global technology leadership, although through different means. A primary method has been an investigation of China's technology practices under Section 301 of the Trade Act of 1974. In a report released in March 2018, the Office of the U.S. Trade Representative (USTR) wrote that China is seeking global leadership in a variety of technologies and that the United States needed to maintain leadership in such sectors as semiconductors and integrated circuits.[26] In part because of the findings of the report and because of the general geostrategic competition with China, the Trump administration as of July 2019 had undertaken a process to raise tariffs on numerous Chinese products and had instituted dispute settlement at the World Trade Organization (WTO).[27] It had also considered restricting Chinese investment in the United States, but opted not to target China specifically, instead deciding to strengthen both the process for reviewing security implications of foreign investment and export controls.

The focus on China comes in the wake of a major new policy document from that country, also focused on triumphing in international competition. In May 2015, China unveiled the "Made in China 2025" document, a ten-year plan, to be followed by two more plans, to "transform

---

[23] President's Council of Advisors on Science and Technology, *Report to the President: Ensuring Long-Term U.S. Leadership in Semiconductors*, Executive Office of the President, January 2017.

[24] President's Council of Advisors on Science and Technology, *Report to the President: Ensuring Long-Term U.S. Leadership in Semiconductors*, p. 7.

[25] President's Council of Advisors on Science and Technology, *Report to the President: Ensuring Long-Term U.S. Leadership in Semiconductors*, pp. 11, 19. Examples of such challenges include quantum computing and point-of-use nanoscale three-dimensional (3D) printing (p. 28).

[26] Office of the U.S. Trade Representative, *Findings of the Investigation into China's Acts, Policies, and Practices Related to Technology Transfer, Intellectual Property, and Innovation Under Section 301 of the Trade Act of 1974*, Executive Office of the President, March 22, 2018.

[27] The White House, "Presidential Memorandum on the Actions by the United States Related to the Section 301 Investigation," Washington, D.C., March 22, 2018; Office of the U.S. Trade Representative, "Following President Trump's Section 301 Decisions, USTR Launches New WTO Challenge Against China," news release, March 23, 2018.

China into a leading manufacturing power by the year 2049," the 100th anniversary of the founding of the People's Republic of China.[28] The plan focuses on ten sectors specifically: "new information technology, numerical control tools and robotics, aerospace equipment, ocean engineering equipment and high-tech ships, railway equipment, energy saving and new energy vehicles, power equipment, new materials, biological medicine and medical devices, and agricultural machinery."[29] For each of these sectors, China intends to improve innovation, integrate information technology, foster Chinese brands, and have greener processes, among other tasks. In sum, the plan has nine tasks, ten key sectors, and five major projects.[30]

There have been instances of cooperation between foreign companies and China regarding Made in China 2025. For example, Chinese Premier Li Keqiang noted the construction of a demonstration production line in Shenyang as a result of cooperation between Germany's Industrie 4.0 plan (that country's plan for digital manufacturing) and Made in China 2025.[31] In addition, there is general agreement that China has every right to aim for technological development and stronger innovation as part of its development process.[32] But foreign countries have been more likely to view Made in China as an attempt to unfairly take global leadership in advanced industries.

For example, the European Chamber of Commerce in China noted that the policy tools to be employed in the plan run counter to fair market competition. These include pressure to turn over advanced technology in exchange for market access, government subsidies to Chinese businesses, and constrained market access for foreign businesses.[33] Likewise, the U.S. Chamber of Commerce contrasts China's plan with Germany's previously mentioned Industrie 4.0, because the Chinese plan provides preferences to domestic industry whereas the German plan does not.[34] The U.S. Chamber of Commerce cites three characteristics of the 2025 plan: (1) reinforcing government control of important parts of the economy, (2) intensifying preferences for domestic industry, and (3) targeting global market share. The end result is to "leverage the power of the state to alter competitive dynamics in global markets in industries core to economic competitiveness."[35]

---

[28] "'Made in China 2025' Plan Revealed," *Xinhua*, May 19, 2018.

[29] "'Made in China 2025' Plan Revealed."

[30] "'Made in China 2025' Plan Revealed."

[31] Li Keqiang, "China and Germany: Building a Golden Partnership on Innovation," speech at the China-Germany Forum: Shaping Innovation Together, Berlin, June 1, 2017. For more on Industrie 4.0, see European Commission, "Germany: Industrie 4.0," *Digital Transformation Monitor*, January 2017.

[32] U.S. Chamber of Commerce, *Made in China 2025: Global Ambitions Built on Local Protections*, Washington, D.C.: United States Chamber of Commerce, 2017.

[33] European Chamber, *China Manufacturing 2025: Putting Industrial Policy Ahead of Market Forces*, Beijing: European Union Chamber of Commerce in China, 2017.

[34] U.S. Chamber of Commerce, *Made in China 2025*, p. 6.

[35] U.S. Chamber of Commerce, *Made in China 2025*, pp. 6–7.

So it is clear that all major economies aim in one way or another to advance their industries, particularly technology industries. Businesspeople and policymakers from Europe and the United States would say that their methods are market-based and provide for fair competition, whereas Chinese methods do not. The Chinese may differ in this assessment. The additional question about all of these plans is whether they actually work, serve as wasteful distractions, or come somewhere in the middle.

Made in China 2025 is not the only grand plan from China. Consider a brief case study of artificial intelligence (AI) in China. Following the release of Made in China 2025, the State Council in 2017 released a national strategy for the development of AI. It called for China to become "a global innovation center" by 2030.[36] According to one translation of the State Council document, the hope is to develop a first-mover advantage, "lead the artificial intelligence development trend of the world, serve . . . economic and social development, support national security, and promote the overall competitiveness of the country and leapfrog development."[37] (Notably, the United States, the European Union, Japan, and the United Kingdom also have plans related to AI.)[38]

Some analysts and technologists in the United States say they believe China can succeed at attaining AI leadership. For example, one characterized China's AI efforts as "the first credible threat to United States technological supremacy since the Soviet Union."[39] He called for significant increases in U.S. funding of research and development. Another author noted that by early 2018, China's efforts had advanced dramatically, featuring a close partnership between state support and businesses. But the author did note that it is not at all certain that China will succeed in its AI ambitions.[40]

And that is exactly right—there is no way to tell whether China will succeed and even whether the Chinese system of politics and economics can lead the world in an innovative area. A recent analysis of China's AI efforts casts some doubts.[41] Consider four factors necessary for AI development: (1) hardware, specifically chips; (2) data; (3) research and algorithm development; and (4) a commercial AI ecosystem. Advancing in each of these areas involves

---

[36] State Council of the People's Republic of China, "China Issues Guidelines on Artificial Intelligence Development," July 20, 2017.

[37] State Council of the People's Republic of China, *Notice of the State Council Issuing the New Generation of Artificial Intelligence Development Plan*, State Council Document [2017] No. 35, Beijing, translated by Flora Sapio, Weiming Chen, and Adrian Lo for the Foundation for Law and International Affairs, July 8, 2017.

[38] Jeffrey Ding, *Deciphering China's AI Dream: The Context, Capabilities, and Consequences of China's Strategy to Lead the World in AI*, Governance of AI Program, Future of Humanity Institute, University of Oxford, March 2018, pp. 11–12.

[39] Adam Segal, "China's Artificial Intelligence Strategy Poses a Credible Threat to U.S. Tech Leadership," *Net Politics Blog*, Council on Foreign Relations, December 4, 2017.

[40] Elsa Kania, "China's AI Agenda Advances," *The Diplomat*, February 14, 2018.

[41] This and subsequent paragraphs draw from Ding, *Deciphering China's AI Dream*.

state subsidies and encouragement, foreign alliances and acquisitions, and training and attraction of talent, among other actions.

This analysis finds that China lags the United States on every driver except for availability of data. And for this factor to provide a meaningful edge, data would have to be more than four times as important as the other three factors in AI development.

In each area, China lags in different ways. And even the data edge is not clear. For example, despite significant efforts and advances at chip development, including state-directed theft of intellectual property (IP), China still lags well behind in certain types of hardware needed for AI and is thus dependent on foreign supplies.[42] China's data policies cut it off from global data sharing, which may prove important to international AI development efforts. Even with its sizable production of technologists and scientists, China as of early 2018 had only about half the pool of AI researchers that the United States had.[43] And even though China's commercial ecosystem is well funded, the number of high-quality start-ups appears to be well below that in the United States.[44] Given global complaints about China's technology-acquisition and IP practices, and suspicions about China's intentions, it will likely be easier for U.S., European, and Japanese firms to collaborate internationally on AI than it will be for Chinese firms.

China's efforts at AI leadership, U.S. efforts at directed semiconductor leadership, and the efforts of other countries to retain or develop leadership in technologies via a coordinated, whole-of-society plan raises the question of whether these plans actually work. There is still tremendous disagreement about where truly breakthrough innovations come from.

There appears to be widespread agreement that broader factors related to the organization of an economic system are important, rather than specific investments for specific technologies. One of these factors has become known as a national innovation system.[45] Although there are efforts to help countries develop innovation systems, there is a lack of agreement about the content of those systems. One study of breakthrough innovations in the United States between 1970 and 2006 found that behind such innovations were networks of organizations and government financing, although the latter has been highly decentralized rather than being delivered as part of top-down, coordinated plans. Over time, the importance of start-up firms increased. And the division between basic and applied science appears to not be relevant, with some basic scientific discoveries rapidly transforming into commercial applications and work on applied problems generating basic scientific discoveries.[46]

---

[42] Ding, "Deciphering China's AI Dream," pp. 23–24.

[43] Ding, p. 26.

[44] Ding, p. 27.

[45] Organisation for Economic Co-operation and Development, *National Innovation Systems*, Paris: OECD, 1997.

[46] Fred Block and Matthew R. Keller, "Where Do Innovations Come From? Transformations in the U.S. Economy, 1970–2006," in *Knowledge Governance: Reasserting the Public Interest*, Leonardo Burlamaqui, Ana Celia Castro, and Rainer Kattel, eds., London: Anthem Press, 2011.

A second broad factor is the receptivity of the economy and society to new innovations.[47] In the words of economist Fredrik Erixon:

> The concept of innovation has basically two elements. The first one is technology creation; that we have scientists and inventors that generate new and bold inventions that are going to help to solve problems in better ways. . . . But the other component of innovation, following the concept of innovation from economists Joseph Schumpeter and many others, is about the economy, and it's about the capacity of the economy to basically take the technologies that are being created and run with them and make them basically ripple through the economy in a way which forces everyone—labor, capital, investors, governments—to perform better.[48]

And that type of absorption has less to do with direct government investments and programs regarding specific technologies and more to do with the degree of competition among firms, the concentration of ownership, the nature of the ownership of firms—financial institutions versus owner-operators who have a greater tolerance for uncertainty and a better understanding of the operations of the firm, and even the pace of new firm formation.

Other factors related to the overall business environment are important.[49] They include laws regarding firm formation and, perhaps counterintuitively, dissolution. For example, regarding firm formation, fewer procedures and lower capital requirements are positively related to new business formation.[50] While bankruptcy laws make it easier to close a business and lay off the workers in that business, they also make it easier to reallocate capital and skills to better uses.[51] Across countries, bankruptcy laws that are more friendly to entrepreneurs are associated with higher rates of new firm entry.[52]

In the 2019 World Bank *Doing Business* rankings, Japan, the United States, and six EU countries are ranked among the ten best in term of resolving insolvency.[53] An additional 11 EU members are ranked between 11 and 30, including the United Kingdom, France, and Italy—the

---

[47] James Pethokoukis, "Is Our Economy Still Dynamic? A Long-Read Q&A with Economist Fredrik Erixon," *AEIdeas Blog*, August 4, 2017.

[48] Pethokoukis, "Is Our Economy Still Dynamic?"

[49] Simeon Djankov, Caralee McLiesh, and Rita Maria Ramalho, "Regulation and Growth," *Economics Letters*, Vol. 92, No. 3, September 2006, pp. 395–401.

[50] World Bank, *Doing Business 2019: Training for Reform*, Washington, D.C.: The World Bank, 2019.

[51] Thomas H. Jackson and David A. Skeel, Jr., "Bankruptcy and Economic Recovery," University of Pennsylvania Law School, July 1, 2013.

[52] Seung-Hyun Lee et al., "How Do Bankruptcy Laws Affect Entrepreneurship Development Around the World?," *Journal of Business Venturing*, Vol. 26, No. 5, September 2011, pp. 505–520.

[53] Resolving insolvency measures the "time, cost, outcome, and recovery rate for a commercial insolvency and the strength of the legal framework for insolvency" (World Bank, *Doing Business 2019: Training for Reform*, p. 23). In this category for 2019, Japan is ranked number one; Finland (an EU member) is second; the United States third; Germany (EU) fourth; Norway fifth; and Denmark, Netherlands, Belgium, and Slovenia (all EU) are ranked six through nine. Puerto Rico as a separate economy is ranked ten, and then Korea is ranked eleven, the tenth-ranked national economy.

largest economies aside from Germany. China is ranked 61. Moreover, in China, with state-owned industry and strong government involvement even in at least some portion of the private sector, businesses can be subsidized beyond the point of economic efficiency and never go bankrupt. One outcome is what has come to be known as zombie firms—firms that without government support would go bankrupt. In China, support for these firms leads to misallocation of capital, higher levels of nonperforming loans at banks, and lower opportunity for more efficient private-sector firms.[54]

In sum, regardless of whether countries would be better off by supporting specific innovations, the fact is that they do compete to develop leadership in technology areas. But there are indications that this type of competition is less important than domestic economic and social policies that lead to innovation networks and partnerships and that foster competition and absorption of innovations in the economy.

Standard Setting

Countries compete directly to expand market share in technology industries. But they also compete indirectly through regulations and standard setting. Regulations, standards, and testing and certification procedures that affect one country's ability to trade with another are known as technical barriers to trade.[55] Such actions go beyond technology and can affect large parts of the global economy. Two factors characterize economies that have power in setting regulations with extraterritorial effect: mandatory for any company selling into a market and, in setting technical standards, generally voluntary. First, it helps to be a major importer. A major importer can require that any company selling to it must meet certain standards. Second, it helps to be willing to set stringent standards. Although such standards may not be economically optimal, when combined with a large market they can have large effects.

The European Union meets both of those conditions, and the result is that products that are made in the United States meeting U.S. regulations and nonregulatory standards may need to be retested and recertified to qualify for sales in the EU.[56] An example of a regulation that has extraterritorial effect for any company that wants to export to the European Union is food traceability, the tracking of any type of food through production, processing, and distribution.[57]

---

[54] Yuyan Tan, Yiping Huang, and Wing Thye Woo, "Zombie Firms and the Crowding-Out of Private Investment in China," *Asian Economic Papers*, Vol. 15, No. 3, Fall 2016, pp. 32–55; Guanjun Shen and Binkai Chen, "Zombie Firms and Over-Capacity in Chinese Manufacturing," *China Economic Review*, Vol. 44, July 2017, pp. 327–342; Wing Thye Woo, "China's Soft Budget Constraint on the Demand-Side Undermines Its Supply Side Structural Reforms," *China Economic Review*, October 6, 2017.

[55] World Trade Organization, *Technical Barriers to Trade*, The WTO Agreements Series, Geneva: WTO, 2014.

[56] Export.gov, "European Union—Standards for Trade," *European Union Country Commercial Guide*, July 19, 2017.

[57] European Commission, "Food Traceability," Factsheet, Directorate-General of Health and Consumer Protection, 2007.

In the automobile industry, there are both small and large differences. European license plates are different from American license plates, so bumper size must be adjusted for cars made in the United States. Unlike the European Union, the United States requires energy absorbers in the roof for protection in accidents, so cars made in the EU must be varied to meet U.S. standards.[58] Requirements for different safety labeling are estimated to cost U.S. chemical exporters about $475 million each year.[59]

All members of the WTO are bound by an agreement on technical barriers to trade. It highlights the goal of avoiding unnecessary barriers to trade and encourages the use of international standards. It recognizes that regulatory and other measures achieve public policy goals, including protecting health and the environment, but they can also be used to limit international competition.[60] Because of these multiple purposes, and because such measures are often complex, nontariff barriers under the guise of standard setting can favor domestic producers that already comply with standards without necessarily triggering retaliation for anticompetitive trade practices.

In the United States, the European Union, and other Western economies, standards are often set by industry groups or independent standards bodies. Internationally, standards are set by the International Organization for Standardization, the standards of which are often the basis for national or regional standards. Besides the European Union, major standard setters are the United States, the United Kingdom, and Germany.[61]

Because of the effect standards may have on the competitiveness of firms, China has been increasing its participation in global standards-setting bodies.[62] Rather than relying on voluntary standards developed by the private sector, China's standards-setting efforts tend to be state-led and regulation-based, meaning the standards are mandatory. There are a number of possible implications for competition. One is that the standards may lower the royalty rates for foreign IP.[63] Others have to do with China's Belt and Road Initiative (originally known as One Belt One Road, and still known as that in China), the agglomeration of policies, goals, and activities aimed at connecting much of Eurasia with Africa and Europe. There, China's activities may lead to the adoption of Chinese standards for construction and data management, affecting non-Chinese companies that want to take part in the Belt and Road Initiative.[64]

---

[58] Emre Peker, "U.S., EU Trade Teams Seek Fast Results and Big Savings," *Wall Street Journal*, October 21, 2018.

[59] Peker, "U.S., EU Trade Teams."

[60] World Trade Organization, *Technical Barriers to Trade*.

[61] FIPRA International, "Standard Setting in a Changing Global Landscape," Report to the European Round Table of Industrialists, October 2010.

[62] Dan Breznitz and Michael Murphree, *The Rise of China in Technology Standards: New Norms in Old Institutions*, Research Report Prepared on Behalf of the U.S.-China Economic and Security Review Commission, January 16, 2013.

[63] Breznitz and Murphree, *The Rise of China in Technology Standards*, p. 32.

[64] Andrew Polk, "China Is Quietly Setting Global Standards," *Bloomberg*, May 6, 2018.

Concluding Thoughts on Competition Beyond Competitiveness

Countries view competition in the global economy as fundamental to their future prosperity. Often, this competition focuses on particular markets or industries, especially high-technology industries. This competition is often couched in terms of global technology leadership and global market share. Countries may also focus on standards, either directly to help their industries or to meet other goals, with the indirect effect of helping their industries. Market share is well defined for specific products. But leadership in a particular technology area is less well defined. The final arbiter of leadership remains the ability of a country to foster domestic economic growth that results in broad-based benefits. This suggests that despite a great focus on international competition, domestic economic policies regarding such mundane matters as efficient government spending, effective training programs, robust infrastructure, supportive education policies, reasonable immigration policies, and sensible regulatory regimes retain primacy in affecting economic power.

Chapter 4. Geopolitical Competition with Economic Tools

Economics as a field of competition involves not only the search for growth and markets. It also includes using economic tools to further geopolitical goals. These uses have been dubbed by one set of analysts, one with longtime foreign policy experience, as geoeconomics.[1] They clearly rest in the realm of competition as action. To be clear, this is not the use of economic tools to improve a nation's economy. Rather, it is "the use of economic instruments to promote and defend national interests, and to produce advantageous geopolitical outcomes" as well as "the effects of other nations' economic actions on a country's geopolitical goals."[2] This chapter covers several of these tools, including sanctions, aid, and other select policies. Chapter 5 takes a broader look at economic competition that may be considered geoeconomics as well.

Using Economics to Punish

Nations have a variety of economic tools to use for geopolitical leverage. A wide range of economic actions fall under the category of sanctions, in which one nation bars certain economic transactions with another. Sanctions are not an end in themselves. They can be instituted to achieve four possible outcomes: compliance, to bring about a behavioral or policy change; subversion, to destabilize or remove a government or regime; deterrence, to stop a country from taking a specific action; and symbolism, to send a message to an international or even domestic audience.[3] Generally, sanctions are not meant to be permanent but to have a specific effect.

But economic actions can go beyond sanctions. Sanctions should be differentiated from other actions to harm an economy (economic warfare) or economic actions in war, such as blockading a country or bombing its ports and factories. Like all instruments of power, economic instruments can be covert or overt. They are more effective if instituted by a dominant economy. They are more effective if instituted multilaterally. By themselves, they rarely lead to victory in wartime, but they can influence the policies of targets and, in wartime, degrade an adversary's capabilities.

The most basic economic action a nation can take is to limit trade. Such trade sanctions can be targeted at a particular sector or a particular country. They can be instituted by a single country or multilaterally. They can bar exports or imports. And they can be offensive or retaliatory. In most cases, they are aimed at shaping or changing behavior. Trade sanctions need

---

[1] Robert D. Blackwill and Jennifer M. Harris, "The Lost Art of Economic Statecraft: Restoring an American Tradition," *Foreign Affairs*, March/April 2016.

[2] Robert D. Blackwill, "Indo-Pacific Strategy in an Era of Geoeconomics," keynote speech at the Japan Forum on International Relations Conference, Tokyo, July 31, 2018.

[3] Michael J. Meese, Suzanne C. Nielsen, and Rachel M. Sondheimer, *American National Security*, 7th ed., Baltimore: Johns Hopkins University Press, 2018.

not involve only goods. Travel is a form of services trade, and travel bans on specific individuals are a standard economic action. An embargo constitutes an act of instituting comprehensive trade sanctions. In this case, all trade with the target country would be prohibited.

Just as countries can limit trade, they can ban investment, either inward or outward. In regulating inward investment, countries can take actions to guard against the offensive use of investment, such as investment to acquire goods or knowledge that may build military capabilities. The most well-known example of investment actions, although not sanctions, is the Committee on Foreign Investment in the United States, which reviews foreign acquisitions in the United States and can negotiate modifications to acquisition deals or recommend they be blocked completely if they represent a security threat.[4] Other forms of investment-related actions include blocking the remittance of profits or interest, blocking the repatriation of capital, and expropriating investments.

One contentious aspect of investment sanctions—and potentially of trade sanctions as well—is that they can sometimes have extraterritorial effect. For example, a proposed U.S. ban on investment in Russian energy export pipelines would affect European companies building Nord Stream 2, a gas export pipeline from Russia to Germany.[5] This is also an issue with financial sanctions.

Related to investment sanctions, financial sanctions block financial relations with the target of the economic action. With the dollar serving as the global reserve currency and the main currency for international trade, the United States is in an unparalleled position to impose financial sanctions. But it is not the only nation that can do so. Financial sanctions can be extraordinarily invasive. The United States can block an institution's access to the U.S. financial system, effectively cutting it off from the international financial system because other banks will be reluctant to do business with it, and largely cutting it off from the use of the dollar to settle international transactions. In 2005, in an effort to affect North Korea's behavior, the United States blocked Macao-based, North Korea–linked Banco Delta Asia from the U.S. financial system, leading most banks to cease doing business with it. The bank, which facilitated transactions for North Korea, collapsed. After a series of negotiations, North Korea returned to multilateral denuclearization talks.

This financial cutoff can also extend to entire countries, and such a cutoff is more effective when it is multilateral. Sanctions against Iran in the period before the negotiation of the Joint Comprehensive Plan of Action provide the best example of such comprehensive, multilateral financial sanctions.

Many sanctions are overt: The sanctioning country states what it is doing and attempts to get other countries to join. Economic actions can sometimes be taken overtly but deniably—that is,

---

[4] Committee on Foreign Investment in the United States, *Annual Report to Congress, Report Period: CY 2015*, Public/Unclassified Version, Washington, D.C.: U.S. Department of the Treasury, 2017.

[5] "Germany Urges EU to Fight Back Against Russia Sanctions Bill," Radio Free Europe/Radio Liberty, August 1, 2017.

they are publicly stated not to be economic actions. China has carried out a number of those types of actions. For example, during heightened tensions between China and Japan in 2010, China blocked the export of rare earth elements to Japan but denied any embargo existed. Filing an official pronouncement could have invited a case before the World Trade Organization.[6]

Another such case occurred in 2016, when the Dalai Lama, the spiritual leader of Tibetan Buddhism, visited Mongolia. Because the Dalai Lama also represents the interests of those opposed to Chinese rule over Tibet, China considers him a "splittist," a "jackal," and a "wolf in sheep's clothing."[7] After the 2016 visit, Chinese border towns raised transport fees on copper and coal from Mongolia, leading to the suspension of shipments from a major Mongolian copper mine. Subsequently, China closed border entries. In neither case did China cite the visit as the cause; instead, a provincial document noted that the surcharges were levied to pay for port infrastructure construction and maintenance.[8]

From Punishment to Economic Warfare

Economic actions used to coerce can accumulate and become economic warfare. The line between the two is not distinct. One definition of economic warfare is "the conscious attempt to enhance the relative economic, military, and political position of a country through foreign economic relations."[9] This author notes that three important points are that actions are purposeful, that they are aimed at a country's relative position, and that they are in no way guaranteed to succeed. Another definition is an "intense, coercive disturbance of the economy of an adversary state, aimed at diminishing its power," again highlighting goals beyond economic.[10] Although actions may be taken against noneconomic assets, economic warfare is most often designed to weaken an economy with the effect of reducing an adversary's political and military power.[11]

Although the goals of economic warfare are different from the goals of economic competition, in that they include military and political goals rather than just economic goals, many of the tools are the same. Economic warfare can include limitations to trade and investment, travel bans, and in the case of actions instituted by the United States, limitations to the use of the dollar and the U.S. financial system. But they can go well beyond these tools.

---

[6] Keith Bradsher, "Amid Tension, China Blocks Vital Exports to Japan," *New York Times*, September 22, 2010.

[7] Andrew Jacobs, "China Attacks Dalai Lama in Online Outburst," *New York Times*, March 24, 2012.

[8] Lucy Hornby, "Rio Tinto Suspends Shipments from Mongolia Mine," *Financial Times*, December 2, 2016; Janice Williams, "China Dalai Lama Conflict: Mongolian Border 'Blocked' Following Tibetan Spiritual Leader's Visit," *International Business Times*, December 14, 2016.

[9] Robert Loring Allen, "State Trading and Economic Warfare," *Law and Contemporary Problems*, Vol. 24, No. 2, Spring 1959, p. 259.

[10] Tor Egil Førland, "The History of Economic Warfare: International Law, Effectiveness, Strategies," *Journal of Peace Research*, Vol. 30, No. 2, 1993, p. 151.

[11] George Shambaugh, "Economic Warfare," *Encyclopaedia Britannica*, July 20, 1998.

For example, sanctions or embargoes to limit trade were described previously. In many cases, these actions may prohibit trade between the nationals of the sanctioning country and nationals of the sanctioned country. In other cases, they may prohibit trade by third parties with the sanctioned country, although this act becomes more difficult to enforce. A more invasive step would be a blockade, in which trade is physically stopped, thereby extending to all countries attempting to trade with the targeted country. A blockade is considered an act of war and is often used in wartime.[12] Other more overt acts of economic warfare could include bombing of factories or other economic assets, as the Allied powers did to Germany and Japan in World War II.

Economic actions can sometimes be taken covertly or deniably, and such actions against an economic target illustrate the porous line between hampering a country's economy as part of economic competition and attempting to achieve political or military goals. In 2015, a cyberattack on three Ukrainian electricity distribution companies caused 225,000 customers to lose power.[13] Although the cause has not been openly proved, Ukrainian and U.S. officials attributed the attack to Russia.[14] Russia more than a year earlier had annexed the Ukrainian territory of Crimea and sparked a separatist war in eastern Ukraine. As of summer 2019, the two countries were still at war.

Such attacks need not occur against an economic target, such as an electricity grid, more directly illustrating the idea that economic warfare includes political and military dimensions. For example, Stuxnet, a software virus, surreptitiously penetrated the uranium enrichment centrifuges at Iran's Natanz nuclear facility, causing the programmable logic controllers to manipulate the speed of the centrifuges, which caused their failure. This incident received great public attention in 2010. Hundreds of centrifuges were destroyed for reasons that were not evident to Iran's engineers, setting back the Iranian nuclear program significantly.[15]

Economic warfare may take place in the context of a military conflict, as in Ukraine, or in a situation where there is no military conflict. The parties might not even agree that economic warfare is taking place. For example, Iran has called U.S. actions against it economic war,

---

[12] For an analysis of the law of blockades, see Michael G. Fraunces, "The International Law of Blockade: New Guiding Principles in Contemporary State Practice," *Yale Law Journal*, Vol. 101, No. 4, 1992. For an economic history of blockades, see Lance E. Davis and Stanley L. Engerman, *Naval Blockades in Peace and War: An Economic History Since 1750*, Cambridge University Press, 2006.

[13] Robert M. Lee, Michael J. Assante, and Tim Conway, "Analysis of the Cyber Attack on the Ukrainian Power Grid: Defense Use Case," SANS Industrial Control Systems and Electricity Information Sharing and Analysis Center, March 18, 2016.

[14] Donghui Park, Julia Summers, and Michael Walstrom, "Cyberattack on Critical Infrastructure: Russia and the Ukrainian Power Grid Attacks," Henry M. Jackson School of International Studies, University of Washington, October 11, 2017.

[15] David Sanger, *Confront and Conceal: Obama's Secret Wars and Surprising Use of American Power*, New York: Crown, 2012, p. 200. Sanger attributes the Stuxnet attack to American and Israeli intelligence, but the source of the cyberattack has never been officially confirmed.

although the United States has not identified its actions as such.[16] Economic warfare can also be considered one set of actions in *hybrid warfare*.[17] Hybrid warfare is conflict across a range of activities, including conventional warfare, irregular tactics, terrorist acts, and criminal disorder.[18]

Despite the destructive effect of the use of tools of economic war, there is little evidence that by themselves they achieve military or political goals when an adversary's core interests are at stake, at least in the short to medium term. However, they can degrade an adversary's capabilities over the longer term and serve as an important contributor to a positive outcome.

Using Economics to Reward

The modern system of international aid arose shortly before the end of World War II with the founding of the World Bank, known formally at that time as the International Bank for Reconstruction and Development. Its initial purpose was to help rebuild Europe, and its first loan went to France in 1947.[19] In the 1950s and 1960s, it shifted its loans to Asia, Latin America, and Africa. Although there was a focus on development, the World Bank and its sister institution, the International Monetary Fund, were also used to reward regimes useful to the West in its Cold War competition with the Soviet Union.[20]

Simultaneous with the growth of multilateral aid, bilateral assistance for developing countries also started rising in the 1950s. In the United States, the 1950 Act for International Development started aid to non-European countries. U.S. officials noted the act was a security measure, saying that U.S. military and economic security depended on the economic security of other countries.[21] The Soviet Union started its own aid program in the 1950s, as did other countries. Various U.S. aid programs were brought together under the U.S. Agency for International Development (USAID) in 1961.[22] But this is not the sole U.S. agency that provides economic assistance. As of 2018, the United States had numerous aid agencies and programs, including USAID, the Millennium Challenge Corporation, the Trade and Development Agency, and even the U.S. Department of Commerce's Commercial Law Development Program, which aims to help developing and post-conflict countries with commercial law development reforms.[23]

---

[16] Babak Dehghanpisheh, "Iran Calls Sanctions 'Economic War,' Says No Talks Until They Are Lifted," Reuters, June 3, 2019.

[17] Przemysław Furgacz, "The Russian-Ukrainian Economic War," *Ante Portas—Studia nad Bezpiecze stwem*, No. 2 (5), 2015, pp. 115–130.

[18] Frank G. Hoffman, *Conflict in the 21st Century: The Rise of Hybrid Wars*, Arlington, Va.: Potomac Institute for Policy Studies, December 2007.

[19] World Bank, "History," 2018.

[20] "Bribing Allies," *The Economist*, September 27, 2001.

[21] David Williams, "The History of International Development Aid," Queen Mary University of London, 2013.

[22] USAID, "USAID History," February 16, 2018.

[23] Commercial Law Development Program, "About CLDP," U.S. Department of Commerce, undated.

Aid measurement and standards started to become formalized with the agreement of a Common Aid Effort by the Development Assistance Group (now the Development Assistance Committee) of what was then the Organisation for European Economic Co-operation (since superseded by the OECD). The commitments about quality and delivery of aid are now generally embodied in the Paris Declaration on Aid Effectiveness and Accra Agenda for Action.[24] Standards include such goals as using aid to fund the strategies that developing countries design, donor country alignment and coordination, keeping procedures simple, and building capacity.

According to development data held by the OECD's Development Assistance Committee, in 2017, countries around the world disbursed $178 billion worth of bilateral official development assistance; multilateral institutions disbursed $41 billion.[25] Official development assistance consists of grants or loans on concessional financial terms offered by governments to promote economic development or welfare.[26]

Among bilateral government donors, the United States was the largest in 2017 at $35 billion, or 19 percent of the total from individual countries, followed by Germany at $25 billion, the United Kingdom at $20 billion, and then Japan and France, both slightly more than $6 billion. Despite these large amounts, they tend to fall short of a generally agreed-on benchmark of 0.7 percent of gross national income (although Switzerland and the United States, among others, do not subscribe to this target).[27] In 2017, for those five largest donors, official development assistance as a percent of gross national income amounted to 0.18 percent for the United States, 0.66 percent for Germany, 0.70 percent for the United Kingdom, 0.23 for Japan, and 0.43 for France.[28]

Two other contributions to international aid are worth noting. First, the United States considers military assistance a form of aid and contends that when all forms of assistance are included, the U.S. aid ratio is larger. Second, nongovernmental and private-sector organizations disburse enormous amounts of aid. Among sources of private financial flows that are accounted for as aid, the United States was by far the largest at $103 billion, well ahead of second-place Japan, at $27 billion.[29] And the United States hosts a large number of nongovernmental organizations that provide aid and assistance. Of almost 315,000 public charities registered with

---

[24] Organisation for Economic Co-operation and Development, "Paris Declaration and Accra Agenda for Action," webpage, 2018d.

[25] Organisation for Economic Co-operation and Development, "QWIDS: Query Wizard for International Development Statistics," undated.

[26] Organisation for Economic Co-operation and Development, "Official Development Assistance," *DAC Glossary of Key Terms and Concepts* 2018c.

[27] Organisation for Economic Co-operation and Development, "The 0.7% ODA/GNI Target—A History," 2018b.

[28] Organisation for Economic Co-operation and Development, "QWIDS."

[29] Organisation for Economic Co-operation and Development, "QWIDS."

the U.S. Internal Revenue Service in 2015, almost 6,700 were dedicated to international causes, with revenues of $38.5 billion and expenses of $34.5 billion.[30]

Despite the Paris Declaration and Accra Agenda, and even though aid has been used to help countries develop, aid has always had foreign policy goals that can be viewed through the lens of strategic competition. Goals have included winning allegiance and obtaining favorable support for donor nations and their policies.[31] U.S. foreign aid historically has had three rationales: U.S. national security, including countering communism, supporting peace initiatives, and countering terrorism; commercial interests, including promoting U.S. exports and improving the global economic environment; and humanitarian purposes.[32]

Europe has also relied on aid for specific purposes. Since 2016, the European Union has increased its aid to Africa in an effort to stem the flow of migrants. The aid is designed with two purposes: to improve conditions in Africa so people do not migrate, and to reward governments that help halt migrants.[33]

Despite the apparent generosity, aid can have negative consequences in terms of political goals. Praising China in 2009 for its investment in Africa, Rwandan President Paul Kagame said, "There is a fundamental problem with development aid. It leads to dependence, the desire of the giving countries to control the receiving countries."[34] He built on this sentiment in 2018 during a meeting with Chinese leader Xi Jinping, saying, "China relates to Africa as an equal. . . . This is a revolutionary posture in world affairs, and it is more precious than money."[35] This statement notwithstanding, it is debatable whether China truly relates to Africa as an equal.

Just as the United States uses aid as a tool in geopolitics, China does as well, and China appears to be expanding its overall aid effort. At the National People's Congress in March 2018, China announced the creation of a new aid agency to coordinate its various efforts.[36] Called the State International Development Cooperation Agency, it is expected to play a strong role in establishing policy for and monitoring China's Belt and Road Initiative, an effort by China to enhance existing policies and expand outreach as part of an overall strategy to develop China's connectivity through Eurasia and Africa to Europe.[37]

---

[30] Brice McKeever, "The Nonprofit Sector in Brief 2018: Public Charities, Giving, and Volunteering," The Urban Institute, National Center for Charitable Statistics, November 2018.

[31] Helen V. Milner and Dustin Tingley, "Introduction," in *Geopolitics of Foreign Aid*, Cheltenham: Edward Elgar Publishing, 2013.

[32] Curt Tarnoff and Marian L. Lawson, "Foreign Aid: An Introduction to U.S. Programs and Policy," Report for Congress R40213, Congressional Research Service, April 25, 2018.

[33] Daniel Mützel, "EU Set to Spend €62 Billion on Africa to Tackle Migration," *Euractiv*, July 1, 2016.

[34] "Rwanda's Kagame Praises China, Criticizes West: Paper," Reuters, October 12, 2009.

[35] Abdur Rahman Alfa Shaban, "'China Relates to Africa as an Equal'—Paul Kagame," *Africa News*, July 23, 2018.

[36] Simon Denyer, "China Sets Up New Foreign Aid Agency to Better Project Influence Abroad," *Washington Post*, March 13, 2018.

[37] Lisa Cornish, "China's New Aid Agency: What We Know," *Devex*, April 20, 2018.

The uncertainty about the new development agency matches a general uncertainty about China's aid activities. China's definition of aid differs from the OECD definition. In addition, the actual amounts disbursed are not published.[38] China also does not place conditions on aid or finance recipients, unlike Western donors. This has also given it an advantage.

In part because of the opacity, and in part because China has provided assistance to governments shunned by Western donors, aid analysts have expressed concern that Chinese aid facilitates authoritarianism and corruption.[39] China would certainly suggest this is not correct, but it is clear that, as with other countries, China uses aid as a policy instrument.[40] Unlike other countries, it is less transparent about what it does.

Other Economic Tools for Geopolitical Competition

One of the main originators of the current idea of geoeconomics, lists seven tools: (1) trade policy; (2) investment policy, including loans to finance infrastructure for geopolitical benefit; (3) sanctions; (4) cyber tools; (5) aid; (6) financial and monetary policy to make a currency more prominent in the world economy; and (7) energy and commodities production and export policies.[41] Some of these are discussed above, and others are discussed below in a broader context. Three things are noted here. First, cyber can be used not only to damage another country, such as by knocking out its electricity grid, as Russia is alleged to have done to Ukraine in 2015.[42] It can also be used to steal intellectual property, technology, and business information, as China is alleged to have done not only to boost its own businesses but to also boost its military capabilities.[43] Second, commodities policies could be similar to trade sanctions, such as when commodities are withheld, but such policies could also involve production to influence global prices, thereby affecting the finances and even stability of other countries. Finally, it should be noted once again that these are policies primarily to influence geopolitical outcomes. In fact, they could be economically costly, and the valid comparison is whether they are more or less effective in terms of costs and benefits compared with other tools.

---

[38] Austin M. Strange et al., "Tracking Underreported Financial Flows: China's Development Finance and the Aid-Conflict Nexus Revisited," *Journal of Conflict Resolution*, Vol. 61, No. 5, 2017, pp. 935–963.

[39] Junyi Zhang, "Chinese Foreign Assistance, Explained," *Order from Chaos Blog*, Brookings Institution, July 19, 2016.

[40] Yun Sun, "China's Aid to Africa: Monster or Messiah?," Brookings East Asia Commentary, Brookings Institution, February 7, 2014.

[41] Blackwill, "Indo-Pacific Strategy in an Era of Geoeconomics."

[42] Andy Greenberg, "How an Entire Nation Became Russia's Test Lab for Cyberwar," *Wired*, June 20, 2017.

[43] Office of the U.S. Trade Representative, *Findings of the Investigation*; Jeff Daniels, "Chinese Theft of Sensitive U.S. Military Technology Is Still a 'Huge Problem,' Says Defense Analyst," CNBC, November 8, 2017.

Economics as a Policy Tool

In the case of sanctions, partly in the case of aid, and partly in the case of other economic actions, countries use economics principally as a tool of geopolitical competition rather than to necessarily foster domestic prosperity. Aid can be related to domestic prosperity to the extent it leads to development in foreign markets or lowers security costs at home. The connections between sanctions and domestic prosperity suggest that, although sanctions may protect the domestic import-competing industry, they will likely increase costs to domestic consumers overall. Sanctions can be effective at damaging the economy of a target country. They are less effective at causing countries to change their behavior, but they sometimes work. Aid is generally thought to help countries develop, at least to a small degree, but does not necessarily buy gratitude or leverage. Other tools may have economic benefits as well: Cyber theft of intellectual property could help the economy of the country doing the theft. Although economic actions, these tools (such as aid and sanctions) are also instruments of statecraft and a way for economics to enter strategic competition among nations.

Chapter 5. Competition over the System Itself

A final major area in which countries compete is in setting the rules under which they compete economically—specifically, the rules of the global trading and investment system.[1] These rules can also have geopolitical effects in the way they create norms of behavior and how they influence political systems. Such competition includes competition as action, but there are also elements of competition as outcome: A positive result would involve the creation of a system that benefits most participants and is attractive enough that countries want to freely participate. The rules-based international economic system established following World War II has accomplished these outcomes and rests on three main pillars. The first is multilateral trade liberalization through what was originally the GATT and is now the WTO. The second is assistance originally for balance-of-payments adjustments and later for all manner of financial and budget crises under the IMF. The third is economic development under the World Bank and regional development banks.

These pillars have supported two simple ideas that have been implemented slowly: International trade and investment should be free among nations, with benefits that are accorded to one partner accorded to all. In addition, businesses of one nation operating in another, either through trade or investment, should be afforded the same treatment as the local businesses in the nation in which they are operating.

The result is a system that has gradually opened to increased trade and investment, allowed reforming countries such as China and the entire former Soviet bloc to take part in opportunities for trade and investment, facilitated rapid growth of international exchange, and enabled a dramatic growth in incomes worldwide.

The United States has been the dominant player in most of the institutions supporting these ideals. The GATT was modeled on reciprocal trade agreements negotiated by the United States in the 1930s, and the United States retains the only single-country veto at both the IMF and World Bank. But as of 2018, the rules-based system is under threat. It has been under modest threat for probably ten years, but in 2018 these threats mounted to a higher level, especially with regard to the trading system.

Even before the Trump administration took office in January 2017, the global trading system faced challenges. In the wake of the global financial crisis, the Group of 20 (G20) leading economies of the world pledged not to resort to protectionism. They have not met that

---

[1] Parts of this material are drawn from Howard J. Shatz, *U.S. International Economic Strategy in a Turbulent World*, Santa Monica, Calif.: RAND Corporation, RR-1521-RC, 2016.

commitment.[2] Since then, the number of discriminatory trade interventions has been in the thousands, with more than 1,000 alone affecting iron or steel products.[3]

The second blow came with the demise of the Doha Development Agenda, a WTO multilateral liberalization negotiation. Trade under the GATT was liberalized in successive negotiating rounds, the last of which, the Uruguay Round, resulted in the founding of the WTO. In 2001, the countries of the world started a new round, the Doha Development Agenda. In December 2015, they ended it without success, the first time such a round has ended with no new deal.[4] But to some, this was more a matter of facing reality rather than taking a bold new step— even in 2011 there was speculation that the negotiating round would not succeed.[5]

Although the failure of the Doha Development Agenda is unlikely to lead to a rollback of trade liberalization, it raises two broad problems. The first is simply the optics that a major multilateral liberalization round failed. Combined with the record of mounting discriminatory trade interventions, as noted above, this heightens concerns that broad-based trade liberalization has not only stalled but may be subtly reversing. The second is that WTO rules are applied differentially to developing countries.[6] As these countries grow faster and achieve a higher share of world GDP and trade, a higher share of world trade will fall under these differential rules if no changes are made to broad-based trade agreements.

In part to seek other ways of shaping the global trading system beyond the multilateral Doha round, nations had been pursuing so-called mega-regional trade deals, which are trade and investment agreements involving large sets of countries but not the entire world. Their effect on future broad-based liberalization is uncertain. On the one hand, they could provide substantial benefits to their members and lower the incentives of these members to seek broader-based agreements. On the other hand, they could prove attractive to countries not yet members and so provide a template for a renewed effort at multilateral liberalization.

Four sets of recent or ongoing trade negotiations are notable for their effect on global trading rules:

- **The Trans-Pacific Partnership (TPP).** This was a trade deal between the United States and 11 Pacific basin nations, including many with which the United States already had trade agreements and two notable countries—Japan and Vietnam—with which it did not. Signed in February 2016, the TPP brought new areas of international exchange under formal rules and set high standards in a number of areas. It excluded China but allowed for the accession of new members. However, during the presidential election, all three

---

[2] Jonathan Lynn, "Protectionism Mounting Despite G20 Pledge: Report," Reuters, June 21, 2010.

[3] For detailed analysis of the wave of protectionism following the global financial crisis, see Global Trade Alert, "All State Interventions Implemented Worldwide Since the Start of the Global Financial Crisis," website, undated.

[4] Shawn Donnan, "Trade Talks Lead to 'Death of Doha and Birth of New WTO,'" *Financial Times*, December 20, 2015.

[5] Alan Beattie, "Doha Trade Round Suffers Fresh Blow," *Financial Times*, July 26, 2011.

[6] World Trade Organization, "Special and Differential Treatment Provisions," Development: Trade and Development Committee, webpage, undated.

candidates with a hope of a nomination—Donald Trump, Hillary Clinton, and Bernie Sanders—came out against the agreement, signaling the United States likely would not participate. During his first week in office, President Trump withdrew the United States from the agreement. In response, the other 11 members continued with the trade pact, eventually signing the renamed and reshaped Comprehensive and Progressive Trans-Pacific Partnership (CPTPP) while leaving the door open to the United States. The CPTPP is considered to be a high-standard agreement setting rules in a variety of areas. In 2016, the 11 countries of the CPTPP accounted for more than 14 percent of global exports of goods and services, so they do have some weight in the world economy.[7] Had the United States joined the agreement, the 12 nations would have accounted for 25 percent of global exports, making the TPP much more influential.

- **The Transatlantic Trade and Investment Partnership (TTIP).** At the same time, the United States was negotiating the TPP, it was also negotiating a trade and investment agreement with the European Union. This likely would have had an even large effect on the future global trading system, since the combined economies accounted for 45 percent of global exports of goods and services in 2016. However, even before it was signed, the agreement met opposition from a number of activist groups in Europe over issues dealing with food and investment arbitration.[8] The agreement was never signed.

- **The Regional Comprehensive Economic Partnership (RCEP).** While the United States was negotiating TTIP, China was leading negotiations for this 16-member Pacific pact. The RCEP was sometimes described as China's way of reshaping the global trading system, or a direct competitor to the TPP, but analysts familiar with trade deals have generally viewed it as having lower standards in the level of liberalization it enforces.[9] In addition, it would have had less weight in the world than the TPP. Combined, the 16 RCEP negotiating partners accounted for 28 percent of global exports of goods and services in 2016. In any case, the talks have been stalled. Although agreement might be reached, deep disagreements among some of the partners remain.[10]

- **Various European Union trade deals.** The fourth effort involves the European Union, and this effort might well influence future global trade rules in a substantive way. The EU has been negotiating deals with numerous partners. One, with Canada—the Comprehensive Economic and Trade Agreement—met similar opposition as the TTIP in Europe but was eventually approved. As of early May 2018, a deal with Mexico was being updated, among many others.[11] And in July 2018, the European Union and Japan signed an economic partnership agreement, creating a free trade area on par with the North American Free Trade Agreement (NAFTA), constituted by the United States, Canada,

---

[7] World Bank, World Development Indicators, "Exports of goods and services (BOP, current US$)," variable BX.GSR.GNFS.CD, downloaded May 9, 2018.

[8] Michael Nienaber, "Tens of Thousands Protest in Europe Against Atlantic Free Trade Deals," Reuters, September 17, 2016.

[9] Peter A. Petri et al., "Going It Alone in the Asia-Pacific: Regional Trade Agreements Without the United States," Working Paper 17-10, Peterson Institute for International Economics, October 2017.

[10] Rosalind Mathieson, "Agreeing on RCEP—China's Favorite Trade Deal—Set to Drag into 2018," *Japan Times*, November 14, 2017.

[11] European Commission, "Negotiations and Agreements," webpage, last updated May 2, 2018.

and Mexico.[12] The importance of these deals is that they export European standards. For example, the update with Mexico will include European requirements for geographic indications for food (ensuring that any sparkling wine called "champagne" really comes from the Champagne wine region of France and that any cheese called "parmesan" really comes from the Parmigiano-Reggiano consortium in Italy), something the United States has balked at.[13] These matters may seem small, but there are numerous standards that the European Union could set through its trade deals, which could then give it a more substantial claim of setting the rules of the global system.[14]

As with many other aspects of global economics, the effect of China's growing role in the world economy has the potential to change the institutional foundations of international trade and investment. One area involves the Belt and Road Initiative. Chinese leader Xi Jinping first mentioned the concept of the Belt and Road Initiative in 2013, and the principles and framework were issued in 2015.[15] Somewhere between a concept and a strategy (admittedly a wide range), the idea aims to build connectivity between China and Europe via Asia, the Middle East, and Africa by land and sea. Major concerns about the plan include whether it will result in Chinese control of ports (to the detriment of other countries), unpayable indebtedness on the part of partners, and new standards that favor China.

A second area is in the realm of institutions. China has set up numerous parallel institutions, the most well known of which in the economic realm is the Asian Infrastructure Investment Bank. The older, more established Asian development finance institution is the Asian Development Bank, dominated by the United States and Japan. In contrast, the United States and Japan are not members of the Asian Infrastructure Investment Bank, but that is by their choice. Despite those new institutions, China has not challenged existing institutions and in fact has tried to become more prominent in them: The first non-American chief economist of the World Bank (Justin Yifu Lin) is Chinese, and China has worked to have the International Monetary Fund include the Chinese currency in the IMF's currency basket, known as special drawing rights. Related, the Asian Infrastructure Investment Bank has so far carried out its activities in cooperation with other development banks, jointly financing projects.

The most contentious area of effects on the system is China's efforts to make international institutions accommodate its state-led economic system on an equal basis to market economies. Gaining greater acceptance for state-led economies within the international system could have strongly negative effects on that system. In most capitalism-oriented nations, there is an arm's-

---

[12] European Commission, "EU and Japan Sign Economic Partnership Agreement," news release, July 17, 2018. In 2017, the combined GDP of the EU and Japan was $22.15 trillion, slightly less than that of NAFTA, at $22.19 trillion. However, in 2016, the order was reversed, with the GDP of the EU-Japan combination valued at $21.44 trillion and that of NAFTA valued at $21.24 trillion (World Bank, World Development Indicators, 2019).

[13] Alan Beattie, "How the EU Could Outflank Trump and His Tariffs," *Financial Times*, April 30, 2018.

[14] Robin Emmott and Philip Blenkinsop, "Europe Seeks to Set Global Trade Rules After Trump Steps Back," Reuters, July 27, 2017.

[15] State Council of the People's Republic of China, "China Unveils Action Plan on Belt and Road Initiative," *Xinhua*, March 28, 2015.

length relationship between a government and a private company, and the post–World War II economic system was set up with basic rules under which not every company favored by a Western government succeeded in international competition. And many of the benefits of corporate success to a government are indirect. Export sales by a private company support employment and profits, and the state will benefit from taxes. However, the relationship between a government and a state-controlled company is entirely different. If a state-owned company has export sales, then the state has access not only to capital and labor taxes but also to the full revenues of the firm. This means it will tend to favor the firm in a way that conflates business interests with state interests.[16]

Notably, there is a long-standing school of thought that state control of businesses is actually a risk to peaceful relations among nations: "Once states take over, on an extensive scale, the ownership of the material factors of production within their borders, the distinction between territorial jurisdiction and property disappears and, *for that very reason*, the fact of geographical inequality becomes a permanent cause of disharmony" (emphasis in the original).[17]

So far, China is falling short of having such a state-controlled model accepted by the major economic powers. When it joined the WTO in 2001, China joined as a nonmarket economy with the promise that it would eventually be recognized as a market economy. That would give its trading partners less opportunity to retaliate against unfair trading practices. However, now that the previously agreed-on time has arrived to deem China a market economy for WTO purposes, the three largest market economies in the world—the United States, the European Union, and Japan—have all said they will not yet recognize China as a market economy, blocking it from achieving that status in the WTO.[18] In fact, all three economies decided in late 2017 to confront China about its trade and economic practices, although how this type of coordination will take place is not yet well defined.[19] Regardless, although the system is under challenge, numerous participants appear to want to maintain and strengthen it.

---

[16] The theoretical effect of state ownership on firm performance is ambiguous: The state may suppress investment by state-owned firms to maximize current revenues to the state budget, ultimately leading to the impairment of the firm, or it may take a longer-term view of the firm and ignore quarterly results, running the firm efficiently to maximize long-term profits. However, as laid out by János Kornai in his 1980 book, *The Economics of Shortage*, there are strong reasons to expect inefficiency. The empirical facts are clear. Public enterprises are inefficient compared to private enterprises and often have excess employment and wages to satisfy political concerns (Andrei Shleifer and Robert W. Vishny, "Politicians and Firms," *Quarterly Journal of Economics*, Vol. 109, No. 4, November 1994, pp. 995–1025). Furthermore, firm operating and financial performance tends to improve after privatization, but employment does not necessarily decrease. That is because improvements in firm performance can sometimes support current or even expanded levels of employment; however, if sales do not increase fast enough, employment is likely to decrease (William L. Megginson and Jeffrey M. Netter, "From State to Market: A Survey of Empirical Studies on Privatization," *Journal of Economic Literature*, Vol. 39, No. 2, June 2001, pp. 321–389).

[17] Lionel Robbins, *The Economic Causes off War*, New York: Howard Fertig, 1968; first published in 1939 by Jonathan Cape Limited.

[18] David Lawder, "U.S. Formally Opposes China Market Economy Status at WTO," Reuters, November 30, 2017; "Japan Won't Recognize China as WTO 'Market Economy,'" *Nikkei Asian Review*, December 6, 2016; "EU, China Joint Statement Founders on Trade Status," *Deutsche Welle*, June 2, 2017.

[19] Eliana Raszewski and Luc Cohen, "U.S., EU, Japan Slam Market Distortion in Swipe at China," Reuters, December 12, 2017.

Chapter 6. Economic Competition and the Armed Forces

The measures of economic competition largely focus on the well-being of a country's population, growth of a country's economy, and a country's production capacity. But economic competition is also relevant to the armed forces. The wealth and output generated by economic activity leads directly to the ability of a nation to fund the personnel, equipment, and effective operations of the armed forces and the technological development that can lead to more lethal weapons and operations. To the extent that economic competition, however defined, leads to a larger economy, economic competition can enable larger, more powerful armed forces and underpin increased chances of victory in wartime.

Economic size does not lead automatically to spending on the armed forces of a nation. For example, in 2017, Germany's GDP was almost 19 percent of U.S. GDP, but Germany's spending on defense was less than 7 percent of U.S. defense spending. While the United States spent 3.5 percent of its GDP on defense, Germany spent 1.2 percent. In fact, that year, not a single country in the North Atlantic Treaty Organization (NATO) spent as much on defense relative to GDP as did the United States, and only three spent more than 2 percent: Estonia, Greece, and the United Kingdom.[1] Actual spending is a policy choice. But having a larger economy allows a country to have the option of spending more on its armed forces than other, smaller countries.

This is the case with the United States, the largest economy in the world. In 2017, the United States had military expenditures of almost $610 billion.[2] In contrast, the expenditures of the two main rivals identified in the U.S. National Security Strategy were much smaller. Chinese military expenditures were $228 billion, and Russian military expenditures were $66 billion in nominal terms converted at market exchange rates. The United States, with its larger economy, is able to spend more on defense.[3]

Spending on the armed forces does not correlate perfectly with effective armed forces, but there is good evidence that the two are related. The Meiji Japanese saying, "rich nation, strong

---

[1] Defense expenditures are from North Atlantic Treaty Organization, *Defence Expenditure of NATO Countries (2011–2018)*, Communique PR/CP(2018)091, July 10, 2018. GDP data are from World Bank, World Development Indicators, online database, version updated January 30, 2019. Both are in nominal terms converted to U.S. dollars at market exchange rates.

[2] This paragraph uses military expenditure data from Stockholm International Peace Research Institute, "SIPRI Military Expenditure Database," 2018.

[3] It should be noted that the figures for China and Russia likely underestimate their spending if it were to be converted on a completely comparable basis. This is because wages and some goods and services are cheaper in China and Russia than they are in the United States, so the equivalent of a dollar in those countries can go much further than a dollar in the United States. Nonetheless, even accounting for that, the U.S. defense budget is larger, enabled by the larger U.S. economy.

army," reflects this relationship.[4] Both World War I and World War II offer several lessons on the relationship between economic size and military victory.[5] In both wars, the side that deployed the most warfighters and equipment won, even if some components of each side floundered. For example, in World War I, the Allied powers mobilized 41 million solders, compared with 26 million for the central powers, and the Allied powers produced 125,000 aircraft and 8,900 tanks, compared with 47,000 aircraft and 100 tanks for the central powers.[6] What made this possible was the prewar GDP of each side; the sizes of their economies were more important than territory or population sizes. More money also provided a cushion for wartime errors.

This success is conditional on time and geography, however. A quick, successful strike by an aggressor would limit or perhaps completely halt the richer defending country's ability to mobilize resources and respond to errors in strategy. Furthermore, economic power is not determinative, as exemplified by the stalemate in the Korean War and the ultimate U.S. loss in the Vietnam War. This is especially the case in counterinsurgencies, as exemplified by the War in Afghanistan, which was in its eighteenth year as of fall 2019.

Along with economic size, the overall level of economic development as reflected by per capita GDP appears to be related to success in military conflict. An analysis of hundreds of battles and wars between 1898 and 1987 found that the side with the higher level of economic development consistently outfought its opponents.[7] Economic development brings several benefits. Most important, it provides an advantage in producing better military equipment and better-trained military personnel.[8]

The changing nature of defense procurement also demonstrates the links between economic competition and the armed forces. Although the U.S. armed forces dominated in militarily relevant technology in the decade after World War II, that dominance is now long gone. Instead, for many purposes, the armed forces rely on commercial off-the-shelf technology, not only

---

[4] As cited in Christian P. Potholm, *Winning at War: Seven Keys to Military Victory Throughout History*, Lanham, Md.: Rowman & Littlefield, 2010.

[5] This draws from Mark Harrison, *The Economics of Conflict and Coercion*, Singapore: World Scientific, 2014.

[6] Harrison, *The Economics of Conflict and Coercion*.

[7] Michael Beckley, "Economic Development and Military Effectiveness," *Journal of Strategic Studies*, Vol. 33, No. 1, February 2010, pp. 43–79. The specific test was of a variable called the loss-exchange ratio, the attacker's casualties divided by the defender's casualties, and the determinant being tested was their relative per capita GDPs. In a sample of 223 events, when the attacker's per capita GDP was higher, the defender suffered more casualties relative to the attacker. This is true even after taking defense spending into account. Additional variables included in the statistical test were a democracy indicator, human capital, two measures of civil-military relations, a series of cultural indicators, military spending per soldier, total troop strength, number of tanks, ground-attack aircraft sorties, and the number of artillery tubes engaged.

[8] Perhaps of concern to the United States, one study found that greater economic equality is positively related to victory in war (James K. Galbraith, Corwin Priest, and George Purcell, "Economic Equality and Victory in War: An Empirical Investigation," *Defence and Peace Economics*, Vol. 18, No. 5, 2007, pp. 431–449). Among developed countries, the European Union and Japan tend to have greater equality after taxes and transfers; the United States tends to be more unequal. When factoring in developing countries, China is even more unequal.

because commercial activities are where much of the innovation is taking place, but also because buying from the commercial market (or modifying commercial products) can be cheaper than buying custom-made technology.[9] A stronger economy can fund not only the research, development, and manufacturing activities that result in new technology, but the education and training that provide the workforce and knowledge for the most effective use of that technology.

One other factor that makes economic competition highly relevant for the armed forces is that international security interests may follow international economic interests. This is particularly a concern with China's growth and internationalization.[10] Already, China is the leading trade partner of many countries. Through its Belt and Road Initiative and other efforts, China is offering large-scale financing for beneficial infrastructure with few of the conditions that Western financial institutions normally place on such loans. This could further reorient trade and financial flows, and political orientation could follow. Additionally, China may want to expand its military presence to protect its investments and Chinese nationals working throughout the world. Such activities are not yet a security challenge for the United States but may become one.[11]

---

[9] Jacques S. Gansler and William Lucyshyn, *Commercial-Off-the-Shelf (COTS): Doing It Right*, University of Maryland School of Public Policy, Center for Public Policy and Private Enterprise, UMD-AM-08-129, September 2008. Aside from their academic appointments, Gansler is a former Under Secretary of Defense for Acquisition, Technology, and Logistics, and Lucyshyn is a former program manager and principal technical adviser to the Director of the Defense Advanced Research Projects Agency.

[10] James Dobbins, Howard J. Shatz, and Ali Wyne, *Russia Is a Rogue, Not a Peer; China Is a Peer, Not a Rogue: Different Challenges, Different Responses*, Santa Monica, Calif.: RAND Corporation, PE-310-A, 2019.

[11] Andrew Scobell et al., *At the Dawn of Belt and Road: China in the Developing World*, Santa Monica, Calif.: RAND Corporation, RR-2273-A, 2018.

Chapter 7. Policy Implications for Economic Competition

Countries are competing economically in a variety of ways and are using economic tools to compete in security and geopolitical domains. Does this economic competition matter? Maybe. One way to answer the question is to start with what countries are competing for, how they compete, and whether global competition allows them to meet their goals.

Economic competition under the broad category of strategic competition can have two conflicting goals. The first is to enable domestic economic prosperity. The second is to harness economic tools for geopolitical purposes. Table 7.1 presents the different domains of economic competition—whether their purpose is more to provide for domestic economic strength or to

Table 7.1. Domains of Economic Competition

Domain	Typical Tools	Economic Effect	Assessment
Economic warfare	Sanctions, blockades, and attributed or unattributed attacks on economic targets to achieve economic, military, and political goals	Degrading or destroying an adversary's economic capacity can reduce that adversary's freedom of action	Use of economic warfare is an adjunct to other types of warfare and by itself will rarely achieve military or political goals, at least over the short to medium term
International economic leverage	Foreign aid for the purpose of gaining allies or winning specific policy debates; economic sanctions to shape behavior; other tools for geopolitical purposes	Evidence that these tools can shape behavior, but economic consequences uncertain	Sanctions can be effective in specific cases but often fail to achieve goals; aid leverage mixed; other tools may have high costs
Leading and setting rules of the system	Helping to found and set rules of international economic institutions; issuing global reserve currency; dominating standards-setting organizations; predominant voting share in institutions; leading voice in informal forums	Limited evidence, but available cases suggest system structure can benefit leader and participants	Some systemic roles (reserve currency, leading institutions) provide major competitive advantages
Public-sector competitiveness policies	Public-sector funding of research and development; support for specific industries; national technology and industrial strategies; public-private partnerships	Evidence that broader policies, at least, can generate economic strength	Overall innovation-system investment can make a difference, but targeted, state-led policies can misidentify winners and losers
Domestic economic fundamentals	Fiscal responsibility and health; stable, effective monetary policy; regulatory and tax environment; rules and standards that affect innovation; socioeconomic opportunity; domestic institutions that support effective economic policy	Clear, consistent evidence that these policies are essential to economic strength	The foundation for all effective competition; other areas will not make up for failures in these areas

SOURCE: Author's assessment based on research for this report.
NOTE: The table presents the different categories of economic competition, whether their purpose is more to provide for domestic economic strength or to serve as tools of geopolitical competition, and a brief note on their effectiveness.

serve as tools of geopolitical competition—with a brief note on their effectiveness and an assessment of their value.

One view of economic competition is reflected in the 1990s debates about *competitiveness*, in which countries are competing to offer their residents a decent standard of living and job opportunities. But another way to frame this issue is that countries are endeavoring to create a policy environment that offers residents the chance to have a decent standard of living and job opportunities, and so this is not really much of a competition because it can be positive-sum rather than zero-sum, and all countries could achieve these goals. Achieving these goals is best served through smart domestic economic policy. Accordingly, the policy implication is that policymakers should focus on providing stable fiscal, monetary, and regulatory policies that emphasize long-run economic growth to undergird the overall economic and political strength of the nation.

Countries are competing to open markets for their companies and attract investment. In some cases, this competition is zero-sum. Investment and trade mean little on their own, but they can contribute to domestic prosperity and opportunity, so such competition matters. Countries are also working to ensure the standards that favor their companies are the internationally accepted standards; doing this will enhance the ability of their companies to operate internationally.

The higher-profile competition is for leadership in industries making and using new technologies. Technological leadership competition often takes the form of support for specific technologies or industries. Certainly, such support can create new, leading industries. But even if such targeted investments help attain technological leadership, evidence suggests that much more is needed in terms of both national innovation systems and the country's receptivity to absorb and use new technologies. Accordingly, the policy implication is that policymakers should support general innovation-supporting policies, such as promoting infrastructure, basic research, patent protections, and technology development to support overall competitiveness and should avoid attempting to pick specific winners and losers in sectors or companies.

Where competition is most likely to matter is in setting the rules by which countries trade and invest globally. As of 2018, that was largely a Western-oriented system, featuring equal treatment of foreign companies, the application of tariffs and barriers on a nondiscriminatory basis, and accepted methods of dispute resolution. The global system is now far freer than it had been through most of history, including most of the post–World War II era. However, with countries instituting trade barriers, the United States trying to renegotiate certain aspects of the global trading system, and China aspiring to remake the global system to better serve its interests, the overall system is under pressure. In some ways, Europe is caught in the middle— finding common commercial cause with the United States vis-à-vis China but finding common institutional cause with China vis-à-vis the United States in the desire to uphold global economic institutions, at least for now.[1]

---

[1] This observation is based on interviews conducted with representatives of the European Commission and research organizations in Brussels, Belgium, in April 2018.

Knowledge of which countries have won competition for markets can be gained just by looking at which companies have the largest market share in an industry. Technological leadership is harder to gauge, but such measures as patents and, more important, sales by technology companies can shed light on that. Gauging the results of competition for the overall system will be more difficult but is still possible. For that, the issue will be whether the basic principles of free exchange and fair treatment that have been promoted since the founding of the GATT will be maintained, or whether systems favoring significant state intervention and selective barriers and treatment will emerge. This competition is likely to play out over the next decade or longer, as long as China continues to grow and take a more prominent place in the world economy.

Accordingly, the policy implication is that U.S. policymakers should take advantage of the relative size of the U.S. economy and market share of U.S. companies to drive for international standards in setting the rules of the system so that they are relatively more conducive to the U.S. economy in the long run. At the same time, these rules must also be attractive to other countries so that they join the system rather than defect to either competing systems or attempt to undermine the system.

Geopolitical competition using economic tools can be effective and by one account is growing.[2] However, these tools can also be costly. Through restraints or new regulations on business, they can cause economic performance to decline. In addition, through overuse, they could lead targeted countries to create alternative systems or workarounds, not only blunting their power but potentially diminishing the economic performance of the country using the tools in the first place.[3] Accordingly, like any other geopolitical tool, the costs of using economic tools must be weighed against their benefits. For the United States, at least for now and likely through the next decade (if not longer), economic tools are likely to remain effective, at least as long as the United States hosts the leading reserve currency and the leading financial sector and remains a major trading economy. Accordingly, the policy implication is that policymakers should be judicious in the use of economic tools such as sanctions and foreign aid, recognizing the unintended consequences and costs of using such tools as part of overall geopolitical strategy.

Finally, economic warfare can prove destructive to an adversary's economy, but there is little evidence that, by themselves, tools of economic warfare achieve military or political goals when an adversary's core interests are at stake, at least in the short to medium term. Tools of economic warfare can also invite similar actions in retaliation, a particular concern when aimed at a large economy with which the United States might be interdependent. Furthermore, they can have consequences for noncombatants, including loss of life. However, they can degrade an

---

[2] Robert D. Blackwill and Jennifer M. Harris, *War by Other Means: Geoeconomics and Statecraft*, Cambridge, Mass.: Belknap Press of Harvard University Press, 2016.

[3] Juan C. Zarate, "Harnessing the Financial Furies: Smart Financial Power and National Security," *Washington Quarterly*, Vol. 32, No. 4, October 2009, pp. 43–59.

adversary's capabilities over the longer term and serve as an important contributor to a positive outcome from the point of view of the country conducting economic warfare. Accordingly, the policy implication is that policymakers should treat the tools of economic warfare as they would any other instrument of war, assessing positive strategic effect and potential harm done before deploying them.

In geopolitical competition and warfare, economic tools can serve as an adjunct to U.S. military power; the ability to use them provides one example of why economic competition is relevant to the armed forces. More broadly, economic competition and its goals of positive domestic economic performance have relevance to the armed forces as well. More direct effects include the ability of the United States to appropriately fund its defense and provide the armed forces with the personnel, equipment, and technology needed to protect the United States from present and future challenges. This places economic competition as an essential element in consideration of overall strategic competition, relevant to military and defense planners.

References

Alfa Shaban, Abdur Rahman, "'China Relates to Africa as an Equal'—Paul Kagame," *Africa News*, July 23, 2018. As of August 11, 2018:
http://www.africanews.com/2018/07/23/china-relates-to-africa-as-an-equal-paul-kagame//

Allen, Robert Loring, "State Trading and Economic Warfare," *Law and Contemporary Problems*, Vol. 24, No. 2, Spring 1959, pp. 256–275.

Austrade.gov, "For Australians: How Austrade Can Help Your Business," Australia Trade and Investment Commission, 2018. As of April 11, 2018:
https://www.austrade.gov.au/australian

Baldwin, Richard, *The Great Convergence: Information Technology and the New Globalization*, Cambridge, Mass.: Belknap Press of Harvard University Press, 2016.

Beattie, Alan, "Doha Trade Round Suffers Fresh Blow," *Financial Times*, July 26, 2011. As of May 9, 2018:
https://www.ft.com/content/fd49df96-b7a3-11e0-8523-00144feabdc0

———, "How the EU Could Outflank Trump and His Tariffs," *Financial Times*, April 30, 2018.

Beckley, Michael, "Economic Development and Military Effectiveness," *Journal of Strategic Studies*, Vol. 33, No. 1, February 2010, pp. 43–79.

Blackwill, Robert D., "Indo-Pacific Strategy in an Era of Geoeconomics," keynote speech at the Japan Forum on International Relations Conference, Tokyo, July 31, 2018.

Blackwill, Robert D., and Jennifer M. Harris, "The Lost Art of Economic Statecraft: Restoring an American Tradition," *Foreign Affairs*, March/April 2016.

———, *War by Other Means: Geoeconomics and Statecraft*, Cambridge, Mass.: Belknap Press of Harvard University Press, 2016.

Block, Fred, and Matthew R. Keller, "Where Do Innovations Come From? Transformations in the U.S. Economy, 1970–2006," in *Knowledge Governance: Reasserting the Public Interest*, edited by Leonardo Burlamaqui, Ana Celia Castro, and Rainer Kattel, London: Anthem Press, 2011.

Board of Governors of the Federal Reserve System, U.S./Euro Foreign Exchange, (DEXUSEU), retrieved from FRED, Federal Reserve Bank of St. Louis, undated. As of July 18, 2019:
https://fred.stlouisfed.org/series/DEXUSEU

Boeing, Philipp, and Elisabeth Mueller, "Measuring Patent Quality in International Comparison—Index Development and Application to China," Discussion Paper No. 15-051, ZEW: Zentrum für Europäische Wirtschaftsforschung GmbH, Centre for European Economic Research, July 2015.

Bradsher, Keith, "Amid Tension, China Blocks Vital Exports to Japan," *New York Times*, September 22, 2010.

Breznitz, Dan, and Michael Murphree, *The Rise of China in Technology Standards: New Norms in Old Institutions*, Research Report Prepared on Behalf of the U.S.-China Economic and Security Review Commission, January 16, 2013. As of May 6, 2018: https://www.uscc.gov/sites/default/files/Research/RiseofChinainTechnologyStandards.pdf

"Bribing Allies," *The Economist*, September 27, 2001. As of May 8, 2018: https://www.economist.com/node/800160

Caselli, Francesco, Massimo Morelli, and Dominic Rohner, "The Geography of Interstate Resource Wars," *Quarterly Journal of Economics*, Vol. 130, No. 1, February 2015, pp. 267–315.

Cerf, Vint, "A Brief History of the Internet and Related Networks," Internet Society, undated. As of July 28, 2019: https://www.internetsociety.org/internet/history-internet/brief-history-internet-related-networks

Commercial Law Development Program, "About CLDP," U.S. Department of Commerce, undated. As of May 8, 2018: http://cldp.doc.gov/about-cldp

Committee on Foreign Investment in the United States, *Annual Report to Congress, Report Period: CY 2015*, Public/Unclassified Version, Washington, D.C.: U.S. Department of the Treasury, 2017.

Corak, Miles, "Income Inequality, Equality of Opportunity, and Intergenerational Mobility," *Journal of Economic Perspectives*, Vol. 27, No. 3, Summer 2013, pp. 79–102.

Cornish, Lisa, "China's New Aid Agency: What We Know," *Devex*, April 20, 2018. As of May 8, 2018: https://www.devex.com/news/china-s-new-aid-agency-what-we-know-92553

Dabla-Norris, Era, Kalpana Kochhar, Nujin Suphaphiphat, Frantisek Ricka, and Evridiki Tsounta, *Causes and Consequences of Income Inequality: A Global Perspective*, IMF Staff Discussion Note, International Monetary Fund, SDN/15/13, June 2015.

Daniels, Jeff, "Chinese Theft of Sensitive U.S. Military Technology Is Still a 'Huge Problem,' Says Defense Analyst," CNBC, November 8, 2017. As of September 26, 2018: https://www.cnbc.com/2017/11/08/chinese-theft-of-sensitive-us-military-technology-still -huge-problem.html

Davis, Lance E., and Stanley L. Engerman, *Naval Blockades in Peace and War: An Economic History Since 1750*, Cambridge: Cambridge University Press, 2006.

Defense Advanced Research Projects Agency, "About Us: ARPANET," webpage, undated. As of July 28, 2019:
https://www.darpa.mil/about-us/timeline/arpanet

Dehghanpisheh, Babak, "Iran Calls Sanctions 'Economic War,' Says No Talks Until They Are Lifted," Reuters, June 3, 2019. As of July 28, 2019:
https://www.reuters.com/article/us-usa-iran/iran-calls-u-s-sanctions-economic-war-says-no-talks-until-they-are-lifted-idUSKCN1T42GB

Delgado, Mercedes, Christian Ketels, Michael E. Porter, and Scott Stern, "The Determinants of National Competitiveness," Working Paper 18249, National Bureau of Economic Research, July 2012.

Denyer, Simon, "China Sets Up New Foreign Aid Agency to Better Project Influence Abroad," *Washington Post*, March 13, 2018. As of May 8, 2018:
https://www.washingtonpost.com/world/china-promotes-foreign-aid-bolsters-environment-ministry-in-government-shake-up/2018/03/13/d3c26d94-267a-11e8-ab19-06a445a08c94_story.html?utm_term=.71cf89fc6f8a

Ding, Jeffrey, *Deciphering China's AI Dream: The Context, Capabilities, and Consequences of China's Strategy to Lead the World in AI*, Governance of AI Program, Future of Humanity Institute, University of Oxford, March 2018.

Djankov, Simeon, Caralee McLiesh, and Rita Maria Ramalho, "Regulation and Growth," *Economics Letters*, Vol. 92, No. 3, September 2006, pp. 395–401.

Dobbins, James, Howard J. Shatz, and Ali Wyne, *Russia Is a Rogue, Not a Peer; China Is a Peer, Not a Rogue: Different Challenges, Different Responses*, Santa Monica, Calif.: RAND Corporation, PE-310-A, 2019. As of March 12, 2019:
https://www.rand.org/pubs/perspectives/PE310.html

Donnan, Shawn, "Trade Talks Lead to 'Death of Doha and Birth of New WTO,'" *Financial Times*, December 20, 2015. As of May 9, 2018:
https://www.ft.com/content/97e8525e-a740-11e5-9700-2b669a5aeb83

Emmott, Robin, and Philip Blenkinsop, "Europe Seeks to Set Global Trade Rules After Trump Steps Back," Reuters, July 27, 2017.

"EU, China Joint Statement Founders on Trade Status," *Deutsche Welle*, June 2, 2017. As of May 9, 2018:
http://www.dw.com/en/eu-china-joint-statement-founders-on-trade-status/a-39099535

European Chamber, *China Manufacturing 2025: Putting Industrial Policy Ahead of Market Forces*, Beijing: European Union Chamber of Commerce in China, 2017.

European Commission, *Growth, Competitiveness, Employment: The Challenges and Way Forward into the 21st Century: White Paper*, Luxembourg: Office for Official Publications of the European Communities, 1994. As of April 9, 2018:
https://publications.europa.eu/en/publication-detail/-/publication/0d563bc1-f17e-48ab-bb2a-9dd9a31d5004/language-en

———, "Food Traceability," Factsheet, Directorate-General of Health and Consumer Protection, 2007. As of May 6, 2018:
https://ec.europa.eu/food/sites/food/files/safety/docs/gfl_req_factsheet_traceability_2007_en.pdf

———, "Germany: Industrie 4.0," *Digital Transformation Monitor*, January 2017. As of May 2, 2018:
https://ec.europa.eu/growth/tools-databases/dem/monitor/sites/default/files/DTM_Industrie%204.0.pdf

———, *Investing in a Smart, Innovative and Sustainable Industry: A Renewed EU Industrial Policy Strategy*, COM(2017) 479 Final, Brussels: European Commission, September 13, 2017. As of April 30, 2018:
http://eur-lex.europa.eu/legal-content/EN/TXT/?uri=COM:2017:479:FIN

———, "EU and Japan Sign Economic Partnership Agreement," news release, July 17, 2018. As of August 11, 2018:
http://trade.ec.europa.eu/doclib/press/index.cfm?id=1891

———, "Negotiations and Agreements," webpage, last updated May 2, 2018. As of May 9, 2018:
http://ec.europa.eu/trade/policy/countries-and-regions/negotiations-and-agreements/#_being-updated

Eurostat, "Archive: Foreign Direct Investment Statistics," *Statistics Explained*, March 19, 2018. As of July 22, 2019:
https://ec.europa.eu/eurostat/statistics-explained/index.php?title=Archive:Foreign_direct_investment_statistics

———, "The Net Investment Position of the EU down at €1, 100 Billion," news release 200/2018, December 20, 2018. As of July 22, 2019:
https://ec.europa.eu/eurostat/documents/2995521/9460172/2-20122018-BP-EN.pdf/65ec907b-804c-4f41-b093-976919369ff3

———, "European Union Balance of Payments—Quarterly Data (BPM6) [bop_eu6_qt]," last updated July 10, 2019.

Export.gov, "European Union—Standards for Trade," *European Union Country Commercial Guide*, July 19, 2017. As of May 5, 2018:
https://www.export.gov/article?id=European-Union-Trade-Standards

———, "U.S. Commercial Service User Fees," U.S. Department of Commerce, webpage, February 2, 2018. As of April 11, 2018:
https://www.export.gov/article?id=CS-User-Fees

Export-Import Bank of China, "About the Bank: Brief Introduction," webpage, undated. As of April 11, 2018:
http://english.eximbank.gov.cn/Profile/AboutTB/Introduction/

Ezell, Stephen, "Krugman Flat Wrong That Competitiveness Is a Myth," Information Technology and Innovation Foundation, January 25, 2011. As of April 10, 2018:
https://itif.org/publications/2011/01/25/krugman-flat-wrong-competitiveness-myth

FIPRA International, "Standard Setting in a Changing Global Landscape," Report to the European Round Table of Industrialists, October 2010.

Førland, Tor Egil, "The History of Economic Warfare: International Law, Effectiveness, Strategies," *Journal of Peace Research*, Vol. 30, No. 2, 1993, pp. 151–162.

Fraunces, Michael G., "The International Law of Blockade: New Guiding Principles in Contemporary State Practice," *Yale Law Journal*, Vol. 101, No. 4, 1992.

Furgacz, Przemysław, "The Russian-Ukrainian Economic War," *Ante Portas—Studia nad Bezpiecze stwem*, No. 2 (5), 2015, pp. 115–130.

Galbraith, James K., Corwin Priest, and George Purcell, "Economic Equality and Victory in War: An Empirical Investigation," *Defence and Peace Economics*, Vol. 18, No. 5, 2007, pp. 431–449.

Gansler, Jacques S., and William Lucyshyn, *Commercial-Off-the-Shelf (COTS): Doing It Right*, University of Maryland School of Public Policy, Center for Public Policy and Private Enterprise, UMD-AM-08-129, September 2008.

"Germany Urges EU to Fight Back Against Russia Sanctions Bill," Radio Free Europe/Radio Liberty, August 1, 2017.

Global Trade Alert, "All State Interventions Implemented Worldwide Since the Start of the Global Financial Crisis," website, undated. As of May 9, 2018:
https://www.globaltradealert.org/

Greenberg, Andy, "How an Entire Nation Became Russia's Test Lab for Cyberwar," *Wired*, June 20, 2017. As of September 26, 2018:
https://www.wired.com/story/russian-hackers-attack-ukraine/

Harris, Briony, "China Is an Innovation Superpower. This Is Why," *World Economic Forum*, February 7, 2018. As of July 27, 2019:
https://www.weforum.org/agenda/2018/02/these-charts-show-how-china-is-becoming-an -innovation-superpower/

Harrison, Mark, *The Economics of Conflict and Coercion*, Singapore: World Scientific, 2014.

Hoffman, Frank G., *Conflict in the 21st Century: The Rise of Hybrid Wars*, Arlington, Va.: Potomac Institute for Policy Studies, December 2007.

Hornby, Lucy, "Rio Tinto Suspends Shipments from Mongolia Mine," *Financial Times*, December 2, 2016.

Irwin, Douglas A., *Against the Tide: An Intellectual History of Free Trade*, Princeton, N.J.: Princeton University Press, 1996.

———, "GATT Turns 60," *Wall Street Journal*, April 9, 2007. As of April 26, 2018:
https://www.wsj.com/articles/SB117607482355263550

Irwin, Douglas A., Petros C. Mavroidis, and Alan O. Sykes, "The Genesis of the GATT," Dartmouth College; Columbia Law School, University of Neuchâtel, and Centre for Economic Policy Research; and Stanford Law School, December 19, 2007. As of April 26, 2018:
http://www.dartmouth.edu/~dirwin/docs/Creation.pdf

Jackson, John H., "National Treatment Obligations and Non-Tariff Barriers," *Michigan Journal of International Law*, Vol. 10, No. 1, 1989, pp. 207–224. As of April 26, 2018:
https://repository.law.umich.edu/cgi/viewcontent.cgi?referer=https://www.google.co.uk/ &httpsredir=1&article=1719&context=mjil

Jackson, Thomas H., and David A. Skeel, Jr., "Bankruptcy and Economic Recovery," University of Pennsylvania Law School, July 1, 2013.

Jacobs, Andrew, "China Attacks Dalai Lama in Online Outburst," *New York Times*, March 24, 2012.

"Japan Won't Recognize China as WTO 'Market Economy,'" *Nikkei Asian Review*, December 6, 2016. As of May 9, 2018:
https://asia.nikkei.com/Economy/Japan-won-t-recognize-China-as-WTO-market-economy

Johnson, Boris (Prime Minister, United Kingdom), *PM Address to the Nation: 31 January 2020*, Prime Minister's Office, 10 Downing Street, January 31, 2020. As of March 9, 2020:
https://www.gov.uk/government/speeches/pm-address-to-the-nation-31-january-2020

Jones-Kelley, Adam, "Top Investment Promotion Agencies," *Site Selection Magazine*, May 2016. As of April 11, 2018:
https://siteselection.com/issues/2016/may/top-investment-promotion-agencies.cfm

Juncker, Jean-Claude, "President Jean-Claude Juncker's State of the Union Address 2017," Brussels, September 13, 2017. As of April 30, 2018:
http://europa.eu/rapid/press-release_SPEECH-17-3165_en.htm

Kania, Elsa, "China's AI Agenda Advances," *The Diplomat*, February 14, 2018. As of May 4, 2018:
https://thediplomat.com/2018/02/chinas-ai-agenda-advances/

Kornai, János, *The Economics of Shortage*, Amsterdam: North-Holland Publishing, 1980.

Krugman, Paul, "Competitiveness: A Dangerous Obsession," *Foreign Affairs*, March/April 1994, pp. 28–44.

———, "The Competition Myth," *New York Times*, January 23, 2011.

Lawder, David, "U.S. Formally Opposes China Market Economy Status at WTO," Reuters, November 30, 2017. As of May 9, 2018:
https://www.reuters.com/article/us-usa-china-trade-wto/u-s-formally-opposes-china-market-economy-status-at-wto-idUSKBN1DU2VH

Leahy, Joe, Peggy Hollinger, and Patti Waldmeir, "Boeing Strikes Deal for Control of Embraer Regional Jet Operations," *Financial Times*, July 5, 2018.

Lee, Robert M., Michael J. Assante, and Tim Conway, "Analysis of the Cyber Attack on the Ukrainian Power Grid: Defense Use Case," SANS Industrial Control Systems and Electricity Information Sharing and Analysis Center, March 18, 2016.

Lee, Seung-Hyun, Yasuhiro Yamakawa, Mike W. Peng, and Jay B. Barney, "How Do Bankruptcy Laws Affect Entrepreneurship Development Around the World?," *Journal of Business Venturing*, Vol. 26, No. 5, September 2011, pp. 505–520.

Li Keqiang, H. E., "China and Germany: Building a Golden Partnership on Innovation," speech at the China-Germany Forum: Shaping Innovation Together, Berlin, June 1, 2017. As of January 19, 2020:
http://english.www.gov.cn/premier/speeches/2017/06/03/content_281475675261196.htm

Long, Cheryl, and Jun Wang, "China's Patent Promotion Policies and Its Quality Implications," Xiamen University and Colgate University, January 20, 2017.

Lynn, Jonathan, "Protectionism Mounting Despite G20 Pledge: Report," Reuters, June 21, 2010. As of May 9, 2018:
https://www.reuters.com/article/us-trade-protectionism-idUSTRE65K2GX20100621

"'Made in China 2025' Plan Revealed," *Xinhua*, May 19, 2018. As of May 1, 2018:
http://www.xinhuanet.com/english/2015-05/19/c_134251770.htm

Magnus, George, "Forget Trade Wars, the Real U.S.-China Clash Is a Tech War," *Prospect*, March 26, 2018.

Mankiw, N. Gregory, "Defending the 1 Percent," *Journal of Economic Perspectives*, Vol. 27, No. 3, Summer 2013, pp. 21–34.

Mathieson, Rosalind, "Agreeing on RCEP—China's Favorite Trade Deal—Set to Drag into 2018," *Japan Times*, November 14, 2017. As of May 9, 2018:
https://www.japantimes.co.jp/news/2017/11/14/business/agreeing-rcep-chinas-favorite-trade
-deal-set-drag-2018/#.WvMIuogvyUk

Mazarr, Michael J., Jonathan Blake, Abigail Casey, Tim McDonald, Stephanie Pezard, and Michael Spirtas, *Understanding the Emerging Era of International Competition: Theoretical and Historical Perspectives*, Santa Monica, Calif.: RAND Corporation, RR-2726-AF, 2018. As of November 6, 2019:
https://www.rand.org/pubs/research_reports/RR2726.html

McKeever, Brice, "The Nonprofit Sector in Brief 2018: Public Charities, Giving, and Volunteering," The Urban Institute, National Center for Charitable Statistics, November 2018. As of July 27, 2019:
https://nccs.urban.org/publication/nonprofit-sector-brief-2018#the-nonprofit-sector-in-brief
-2018-public-charites-giving-and-volunteering

Meese, Michael J., Suzanne C. Nielsen, and Rachel M. Sondheimer, *American National Security*, 7th ed., Baltimore, Md.: Johns Hopkins University Press, 2018.

Megginson, William L., and Jeffrey M. Netter, "From State to Market: A Survey of Empirical Studies on Privatization," *Journal of Economic Literature*, Vol. 39, No. 2, June 2001, pp. 321–389.

Menon, Ravi (Managing Director, Monetary Authority of Singapore), "An Economic History of Singapore: 1965–2065," keynote address at the Singapore Economic Review Conference 2015, August 5, 2015. As of March 5, 2020:
https://www.mas.gov.sg/news/speeches/2015/an-economic-history-of-singapore

Milner, Helen V., and Dustin Tingley, "Introduction," in *Geopolitics of Foreign Aid*, London: Edward Elgar Publishing, 2013.

Moss, Todd, and Sarah Rose, "China ExIm Bank and Africa: New Lending, New Challenges," CGD Notes, Center for Global Development, November 2006.

Mützel, Daniel, "EU Set to Spend €62 Billion on Africa to Tackle Migration," *Euractiv*, July 1, 2016. As of August 11, 2018:
https://www.euractiv.com/section/global-europe/news/eu-set-to-spend-e62-billion-on-africa
-to-tackle-migration/

Nienaber, Michael, "Tens of Thousands Protest in Europe Against Atlantic Free Trade Deals," Reuters, September 17, 2016. As of May 9, 2018:
https://www.reuters.com/article/us-eu-usa-ttip-idUSKCN11N0H6

North Atlantic Treaty Organization, *Defence Expenditure of NATO Countries (2011–2018)*, Communique PR/CP(2018)091, July 10, 2018. As of March 11, 2019:
https://www.nato.int/cps/en/natohq/news_156770.htm

Office of Science and Technology Policy, "PCAST Documents and Reports," webpage, 2017. As of April 30, 2018:
https://obamawhitehouse.archives.gov/administration/eop/ostp/pcast/docsreports

Office of the U.S. Trade Representative, *Findings of the Investigation into China's Acts, Policies, and Practices Related to Technology Transfer, Intellectual Property, and Innovation Under Section 301 of the Trade Act of 1974*, Executive Office of the President, March 22, 2018.

———, "Following President Trump's Section 301 Decisions, USTR Launches New WTO Challenge Against China," news release, March 23, 2018.

Organisation for Economic Co-operation and Development, "QWIDS: Query Wizard for International Development Statistics," undated. As of July 27, 2019:
http://stats.oecd.org/qwids/

———, *National Innovation Systems*, Paris: OECD, 1997.

———, "Official Export Credit Agencies," webpage, March 7, 2017. As of April 11, 2018:
http://www.oecd.org/tad/xcred/eca.htm

———, "Income Distribution Database (IDD)," 2018a. As of July 19, 2019:
http://www.oecd.org/social/income-distribution-database.htm

———, "The 0.7% ODA/GNI Target—A History," 2018b. As of May 8, 2018:
http://www.oecd.org/dac/stats/the07odagnitarget-ahistory.htm

———, "Official Development Assistance," *DAC Glossary of Key Terms and Concepts*, 2018c. As of May 8, 2018:
http://www.oecd.org/dac/dac-glossary.htm

———, "Paris Declaration and Accra Agenda for Action," webpage, 2018d. As of May 8, 2018:
http://www.oecd.org/dac/effectiveness/parisdeclarationandaccraagendaforaction.htm

———, "Triadic Patent Families," webpage and database, 2019. As of July 24, 2109:
https://data.oecd.org/rd/triadic-patent-families.htm

Park, Donghui, Julia Summers, and Michael Walstrom, "Cyberattack on Critical Infrastructure: Russia and the Ukrainian Power Grid Attacks," Henry M. Jackson School of International Studies, University of Washington, October 11, 2017. As of July 28, 2019: https://jsis.washington.edu/news/cyberattack-critical-infrastructure-russia-ukrainian-power -grid-attacks/

Peker, Emre, "U.S., EU Trade Teams Seek Fast Results and Big Savings," *Wall Street Journal*, October 21, 2018. As of July 27, 2019: https://www.wsj.com/articles/u-s-eu-trade-teams-seek-fast-results-and-big-savings -1540123200

Pethokoukis, James, "Is Our Economy Still Dynamic? A Long-Read Q&A with Economist Fredrik Erixon," *AEIdeas Blog*, August 4, 2017. As of August 10, 2018: http://www.aei.org/publication/is-our-economy-still-dynamic-a-qa-with-economist-fredrik -erixon/

Petri, Peter A., Michael G. Plummer, Shujiro Urata, and Fan Zhai, "Going It Alone in the Asia-Pacific: Regional Trade Agreements Without the United States," Working Paper 17-10, Peterson Institute for International Economics, October 2017.

Polk, Andrew, "China Is Quietly Setting Global Standards," *Bloomberg*, May 6, 2018. As of May 6, 2018: https://www.bloomberg.com/view/articles/2018-05-06/china-is-quietly-setting-global -standards

Popp, David, "Using the Triadic Patent Family Database to Study Environmental Innovation," Organisation for Economic Co-operation and Development, 2007. As of August 10, 2018: https://www.oecd.org/env/consumption-innovation/38283097.pdf

Potholm, Christian P., *Winning at War: Seven Keys to Military Victory Throughout History*, Lanham, Md.: Rowman & Littlefield, 2010.

President's Council of Advisors on Science and Technology, *Report to the President on Ensuring American Leadership in Advanced Manufacturing*, Executive Office of the President, June 2011.

———, *Report to the President: Ensuring Long-Term U.S. Leadership in Semiconductors*, Executive Office of the President, January 2017. As of May 1, 2018: https://obamawhitehouse.archives.gov/sites/default/files/microsites/ostp/PCAST/ pcast_ensuring_long-term_us_leadership_in_semiconductors.pdf

Raszewski, Eliana, and Luc Cohen, "U.S., EU, Japan Slam Market Distortion in Swipe at China," Reuters, December 12, 2017. As of May 9, 2018: https://www.reuters.com/article/us-trade-wto/u-s-eu-japan-slam-market-distortion-in-swipe -at-china-idUSKBN1E62HA

Ricardo, David, *On the Principles of Political Economy and Taxation*, London: John Murray, 1817.

Robbins, Lionel, *The Economic Causes off War*, New York: Howard Fertig, 1968; first published in 1939 by Jonathan Cape Limited.

"Rwanda's Kagame Praises China, Criticizes West: Paper," Reuters, October 12, 2009. As of March 10, 2020:
https://af.reuters.com/article/worldNews/idAFTRE59B1JS20091012

Sanger, David, *Confront and Conceal: Obama's Secret Wars and Surprising Use of American Power*, New York: Crown, 2012.

Schwab, Klaus, ed., *The Global Competitiveness Report 2017–2018*, Insight Report, Geneva: World Economic Forum, 2017.

Scobell, Andrew, Bonny Lin, Howard J. Shatz, Michael Johnson, Larry Hanauer, Michael S. Chase, Astrid Stuth Cevallos, Ivan W. Rasmussen, Arthur Chan, Aaron Strong, Eric Warner, and Logan Ma, *At the Dawn of Belt and Road: China in the Developing World*, Santa Monica, Calif.: RAND Corporation, RR-2273-A, 2018. As of March 12, 2019:
https://www.rand.org/pubs/research_reports/RR2273.html

Segal, Adam, "China's Artificial Intelligence Strategy Poses a Credible Threat to U.S. Tech Leadership," *Net Politics Blog*, Council on Foreign Relations, December 4, 2017. As of May 5, 2018:
https://www.cfr.org/blog/chinas-artificial-intelligence-strategy-poses-credible-threat-us-tech-leadership

Shambaugh, George, "Economic Warfare," *Encyclopaedia Britannica*, July 20, 1998. As of July 28, 2019:
https://www.britannica.com/topic/economic-warfare

Shambaugh, Jay, Ryan Nunn, and Becca Portman, "Eleven Facts About Innovation and Patents," Economic Facts, The Hamilton Project, Brookings Institution, December 2017. As of August 10, 2018:
https://www.brookings.edu/wp-content/uploads/2017/12/thp_20171213_eleven_facts_innovation_patents.pdf

Shatz, Howard J., *U.S. International Economic Strategy in a Turbulent World*, Santa Monica, Calif.: RAND Corporation, RR-1521-RC, 2016. As of January 19, 2020:
https://www.rand.org/pubs/research_reports/RR1521.html

Shen, Guanjun, and Binkai Chen, "Zombie Firms and Over-Capacity in Chinese Manufacturing," *China Economic Review*, Vol. 44, July 2017, pp. 327–342.

Shleifer, Andrei, and Robert W. Vishny, "Politicians and Firms," *Quarterly Journal of Economics*, Vol. 109, No. 4, November 1994, pp. 995–1025.

Sirkin, Hal, Justin Rose, and Rahul Choraria, "An Innovation-Led Boost for U.S. Manufacturing," Boston Consulting Group, April 17, 2017. As of July 27, 2019:
https://www.bcg.com/publications/2017/lean-innovation-led-boost-us-manufacturing.aspx

Smith, Adam, *An Inquiry into the Nature and Causes of the Wealth of Nations*, London: William Strahan and Thomas Cadell, 1776.

State Council of the People's Republic of China, "China Unveils Action Plan on Belt and Road Initiative," *Xinhua*, March 28, 2015. As of May 9, 2018:
http://english.gov.cn/news/top_news/2015/03/28/content_281475079055789.htm

———, "China Issues Guidelines on Artificial Intelligence Development," July 20, 2017. As of May 2, 2018:
http://english.gov.cn/policies/latest_releases/2017/07/20/content_281475742458322.htm

———, *Notice of the State Council Issuing the New Generation of Artificial Intelligence Development Plan*, State Council Document [2017] No. 35, Beijing, translated by Flora Sapio, Weiming Chen, and Adrian Lo for the Foundation for Law and International Affairs, July 8, 2017. As of May 2, 2018:
https://flia.org/wp-content/uploads/2017/07/A-New-Generation-of-Artificial-Intelligence -Development-Plan-1.pdf

Stockholm International Peace Research Institute, "SIPRI Military Expenditure Database," 2018. As of March 11, 2019:
https://sipri.org/databases/milex

Strange, Austin M., Alex Dreher, Andreas Fuchs, Bradley Parks, and Michael J. Tierney, "Tracking Underreported Financial Flows: China's Development Finance and the Aid-Conflict Nexus Revisited," *Journal of Conflict Resolution*, Vol. 61, No. 5, 2017, pp. 935–963.

Subramanian, Arvind, "Countering China's Economic Dominance," *Business Standard*, January 20, 2013. As of August 10, 2018:
https://www.business-standard.com/article/opinion/arvind-subramanian-countering-china-s -economic-dominance-111082400101_1.html

Sun, Yun, "China's Aid to Africa: Monster or Messiah?," Brookings East Asia Commentary, Brookings Institution, February 7, 2014. As of May 8, 2018:
https://www.brookings.edu/opinions/chinas-aid-to-africa-monster-or-messiah/

Takahashi, Koji, "The Future of the Japanese Style Employment System: Continued Long-Term Employment and the Challenges It Faces," *Japan Labor Issues*, Vol. 2, No. 6, April–May 2018, pp. 6–15.

Tan, Yuyan, Yiping Huang, and Wing Thye Woo, "Zombie Firms and the Crowding-Out of Private Investment in China," *Asian Economic Papers*, Vol. 15, No. 3, Fall 2016, pp. 32–55.

Tankersley, Jim, "Economists Say U.S. Tariffs Are Wrong Move on a Valid Issue," *New York Times*, April 11, 2018. As of August 10, 2018:
https://www.nytimes.com/2018/04/11/business/economy/trump-economists.html

Tarnoff, Curt, and Marian L. Lawson, "Foreign Aid: An Introduction to U.S. Programs and Policy," Report for Congress R40213, Congressional Research Service, April 25, 2018.

Thurow, Lester, "Microchips, Not Potato Chips," *Foreign Affairs*, July/August 1994. As of April 9, 2018:
https://www.foreignaffairs.com/articles/1994-07-01/microchips-not-potato-chips

Tyson, Laura D'Andrea, *Who's Bashing Whom? Trade Conflict in High-Technology Industries*, Washington, D.C.: Institute for International Economics, November 1992.

United Nations Conference on Trade and Development, UNCTADStat, undated. As of July 18, 2019:
https://unctadstat.unctad.org/EN/

United Nations, UN Comtrade Database, 2019a. As of July 24, 2019:
https://comtrade.un.org/data

———, World Population Prospects, 2019b, data query. As of July 18, 2019:
https://esa.un.org/unpd/wpp/DataQuery/

USAID, "USAID History," February 16, 2018. As of May 8, 2018:
https://www.usaid.gov/who-we-are/usaid-history

U.S. Bureau of Economic Analysis, "U.S. Trade in Goods and Services by Selected Countries and Areas, 1999–Present," Excel spreadsheet, last updated June 19, 2019.

U.S. Chamber of Commerce, *Made in China 2025: Global Ambitions Built on Local Protections*, Washington, D.C.: United States Chamber of Commerce, 2017.

U.S. International Trade Commission, *Global Competitiveness of U.S. Advanced-Technology Manufacturing Industries: Semiconductor Manufacturing and Testing Equipment*, Report to the Committee on Finance, United States Senate, on Investigation No. 332-303 Under Section 332(g) of the Tariff Act of 1930, USITC Publication 2434, September 1991.

U.S. Trade and Development Agency, "Our Mission," webpage, undated. As of April 12, 2018:
https://www.ustda.gov/about/mission

Veugelers, Reinhilde, "The Challenge of China's Rise as a Science and Technology Powerhouse," *Brink Asia*, August 28, 2017. As of April 11, 2018:
http://www.brinknews.com/asia/the-challenge-of-chinas-rise-as-a-science-and-technology-powerhouse/

Wang, Dan, "Why China Will Rival the U.S. in High Tech," Bloomberg Opinion, April 25, 2019. As of July 27, 2019:
https://www.bloomberg.com/opinion/articles/2019-04-25/china-will-ultimately-rival-u-s-in-innovation

The White House, *National Security Strategy of the United States of America*, Washington, D.C., December 2017.

———, "Presidential Memorandum on the Actions by the United States Related to the Section 301 Investigation," Washington, D.C., March 22, 2018.

Williams, David, "The History of International Development Aid," Queen Mary University of London, 2013.

Williams, Janice, "China Dalai Lama Conflict: Mongolian Border 'Blocked' Following Tibetan Spiritual Leader's Visit," *International Business Times*, December 14, 2016.

Woo, Wing Thye, "China's Soft Budget Constraint on the Demand-Side Undermines Its Supply Side Structural Reforms," *China Economic Review*, Vol. 57, October 2019. As of March 5, 2020:
https://www.sciencedirect.com/science/article/pii/S1043951X1730144X

World Bank, "History," 2018. As of May 8, 2018:
http://www.worldbank.org/en/about/archives/history

World Bank, *Doing Business 2019: Training for Reform*, Washington, D.C.: The World Bank, 2019.

World Bank, World Development Indicators, online database, version updated July 10, 2019.

World Intellectual Property Organization, "WIPO Statistics Database," last updated December 2018. As of July 24, 2019:
https://www3.wipo.int/ipstats/index.htm?tab=patent

World Trade Organization, "Special and Differential Treatment Provisions," Development: Trade and Development Committee, webpage, undated. As of July 27, 2019:
https://www.wto.org/english/tratop_e/devel_e/dev_special_differential_provisions_e.htm

———, *Technical Barriers to Trade*, The WTO Agreements Series, Geneva: WTO, 2014. As of July 27, 2019:
https://www.wto.org/english/res_e/publications_e/tbttotrade_e.pdf

Yeung, Yue-man, Joanna Lee, and Gordon Kee, "China's Special Economic Zones at 30," *Eurasian Geography and Economics*, Vol. 50, No. 2, 2009, pp. 222–240.

Zarate, Juan C., "Harnessing the Financial Furies: Smart Financial Power and National Security," *Washington Quarterly*, Vol. 32, No. 4, October 2009, pp. 43–59.

Zhang, Junyi, "Chinese Foreign Assistance, Explained," *Order from Chaos Blog*, Brookings Institution, July 19, 2016. As of May 8, 2018:
https://www.brookings.edu/blog/order-from-chaos/2016/07/19/chinese-foreign-assistance-explained/